Adolescents at School

Perspectives on Youth, Identity, and Education

Edited by

MICHAEL SADOWSKI

HARVARD EDUCATION PRESS

Library of Congress Control Number 2002117403
ISBN 1-891792-11-3 (cloth)
ISBN 1-891792-10-5 (paper)

Published by Harvard Education Press,
an imprint of the Harvard Education Publishing Group

Harvard Education Press
8 Story Street, 5th Floor
Cambridge, MA 02138

Cover design by Alyssa Morris
Cover photograph © Corbis

The typefaces used in this book are Sabon for the text and Gill Sans for
the titles. Sabon is a descendant of the types of Claude Garamond. It was
designed in 1964 by Jan Tschichold. Gill Sans was designed by Eric Gill
around 1929. It is based on the typface designed by Edward Johnston in
1916 for the signage of the London Underground.

Adolescents at School

Contents

Why Identity Matters at School

MICHAEL SADOWSKI

Standards, accountability, and testing are probably the three words that best sum up the approach to education reform that currently prevails across the United States. The logic goes something like this: Raise the bar for students and they will perform better. Hold schools accountable and educators will be driven to produce results. Test students to see what they know and are able to do, and both they and their teachers will be motivated to avoid the consequences that come with low scores.

Driven by federal and state initiatives, educators at the district level have had little choice but to tailor their instructional approaches, at least in part, to suit the requirements of the standards-based model. And while this approach to raising student achievement arguably has its merits, educators who focus solely on these factors—factors that are external to their students—are likely to achieve only limited success. The simple reason is that while tests, curricula, and state frameworks can be standardized, students never can and never will be. If we want students to succeed—not just as test-takers but also as thinkers, as learners, and as people who make valuable contributions to our society—we need to know more about them than their scores on standardized measures of achievement.

Collectively, the authors in this volume make a powerful case that much of a student's success or failure in school—academically, socially, and personally—centers not on these external factors but on questions of *identity*: "Who am I?" "What kind of student do I want to be?" "What things are important to me?" "What do others expect of me?" "Where do I want to go with my life?" "How do other people perceive me?" Though perhaps not consciously, these kinds of questions weigh especially heavily on the minds of adolescents, who probably wrestle with them more intensely than any other age group. And, since adolescents spend a major portion of their waking hours in school, middle and high schools are both mirrors and shapers of their identity development experience.

In a standards-driven climate, many policymakers—and perhaps even some educators—might dismiss identity as an academic concept, a term emanating from the halls of the ivory tower that is, at best, peripheral to the "real work" of schools: raising academic achievement. Indeed, many educators first encounter the concept of adolescent identity, as I did, in the coursework of their university-based teacher or administrator training programs. Yet the many adolescents with whom I have worked as a high school teacher, youth advisor, and academic mentor have convinced me that it is as important for middle and high school educators to understand identity as it is for them to understand pedagogy. In order for educators to help adolescents succeed *as students*, we must develop a better understanding of the issues that affect them *as people*. To that end, this book is intended to be highly practical, one that educators, counselors, youth leaders, parents, and others can consult to deepen this understanding.

Last summer, I co-taught an Advanced Placement (AP) transition class for promising students who had not been in upper-level English courses previously, but were planning to take AP classes as juniors. A number of students in the class, many of them African American males, seemed to struggle with reconciling this new "high-achiever" identity with the low expectations they were accustomed to from teachers, administrators, peers, and in some cases themselves. Some of them became comfortable in the role of AP scholar by summer's end, while others decided they weren't ready to do so. Having conversations with my students about these issues helped me to understand why some resisted success despite their skill and promise, and others found the personal resources to forge new identities for themselves as learners.

As an advisor to another high school's gay-straight alliance, I knew a number of lesbian, gay, bisexual, and transgender students who sometimes chose to stay home from school in order to avoid the harassment they experienced there. (At least one student eventually dropped out altogether.) Yet at the same school I also knew sexual minority students who transformed discrimination into a catalyst for activism and a strong sense of purpose in their lives. Issues of identity obviously were important factors in these students' success—or lack thereof—in school and beyond. Similarly, as an English and drama teacher, I had students with disabilities in several of my classes who seemed to believe that they needed to segregate themselves from their classmates and others who viewed themselves, and were viewed by others, as full participants in the school community. Clearly, how these youth incorporated disability into their identities was central to the ways they connected to, enjoyed, and performed in school.

*   *   *

Adolescents at School is a relatively simple title for a book about an exceedingly complex topic. Of course, any volume about the ways identity-related issues affect middle and high school students will inevitably be incomplete, since there are infinite aspects of adolescent identity and infinite ways these can play out in academic environments. Rather than a comprehensive "text" on adolescent identity (which would be impossible to assemble), the book is an invitation to consider a range of related topics in a variety of ways.

Michael Nakkula's opening chapter, "Identity and Possibility," explores the universal adolescent quest for identity by drawing on the classic model of psychologist Erik Erikson.[1] Profiling "Mac," a contemporary adolescent, Nakkula shows how aspects of this widely cited framework apply to youth in today's schools. According to Erikson's model, the identity "crisis" of adolescence is part of a series of developmental transitions that begin in infancy and occur throughout a person's life. In adolescence, questions of identity take on special significance as adolescents try to make sense of themselves, their futures, and their world in the face of pressure from peers, teachers, parents, and others. It is especially important during this stage, Nakkula writes, for adolescents to have opportunities to invest their energies positively in a variety of pursuits, both academic and otherwise. Without such opportunities, youth are at risk of identity "foreclosure," whereby they can become "stuck" in preconceived notions of who they are. This is where educators, counselors, and others who work with and care about youth can play crucial roles: mentoring, counseling, coaching—also just providing space, listening, and allowing adolescents to be themselves. Nakkula ends his chapter by illustrating how schools can be places of possibility, giving youth many opportunities to explore a variety of pathways and answers to the question, "Who am I?"

The chapters that follow are devoted to five aspects of identity that can have especially profound effects on adolescents' school lives: race and ethnicity, gender, sexual orientation, social class, and ability/disability. Though certainly not an exhaustive list of the factors that affect middle and high school aged youth, these issues can be crucial in the development of their sense of self, their social interactions with peers, their relationships with teachers and other adults, their goals and plans for the future, and their academic achievement. They also can be associated with the kind of identity foreclosure against which Nakkula warns. For example, if adolescents view themselves through societal prejudices about what it means to be African American or poor or gay or an immigrant, they may have difficulty realizing their full potential as human beings.

In the book's final chapter, "Beyond Categories," John Raible and Sonia Nieto expand the framework for understanding adolescent identity, profiling three young people whose lives represent the intersection of multiple identities and experiences. As with the adolescents featured throughout the book, these young people demonstrate how factors such as race, gender, sexual orientation, class, and ability—though extremely useful for understanding aspects of the adolescent experience—tell only part of the story, the remainder of which is unique to each individual.

Like the youth and the issues about which they write, the contributors to *Adolescents at School* are a diverse group. The researchers, educators, counselors, and education journalists represented here shed light on adolescents' school lives from a multiplicity of vantage points and use a variety of approaches. Commentaries, interviews, and profiles (of individual adolescents or groups of students) complement each of the longer chapters and provide additional perspectives on the issues raised in them. In many cases, authors draw on the voices of youth themselves, citing the "real authorities" on the adolescent experience in interview excerpts, anecdotes, case studies, and samples of student writing.

* * *

Working with young people in ways that reflect an understanding of some of the identity issues they might experience is distinct from the worthwhile but different goal of helping them build self-esteem. While issues of identity and self-esteem at times intersect at school, they are not one and the same. Like other educators, I have known students who seemed to have high self-esteem despite poor academic performance, as well as high achievers who I believed had low self-perceptions. I am not sure whether the students in my AP transition class, for example, felt good about themselves as people. Despite my hopes for all of them, I suspect that some did and some didn't. (Adolescents can be notoriously self-critical.) As is true of all students with whom we might work, we will never know everything about what they are thinking, how they feel, or how they see the world. But it was clear to me that, for these students, questions of how they viewed themselves as learners at that point in their lives, who they wanted to be, and what others expected of them affected their success in school and, quite possibly, their future life chances. I believe that exploring these questions, as imperfect as my understanding may have been, made me a better teacher.

Standardized tests, state curriculum frameworks, and other accountability-based measures may well have a place in setting baseline levels for the knowledge and skills we want all students to have before they graduate from our schools. But they also carry with them the risk of seeing each student as a number, a percentile ranking along a distribution of test scores, or a member of a group labeled "proficient," "needs improvement," or "failing." To paraphrase Thomas Fowler-Finn, superintendent of the Fort Wayne (IN) Community Schools and a contributor to this volume, improving achievement involves much more than taking measures to raise test scores. It also involves understanding our students' perceptions, how they view their relationships with educators and education, and a host of other factors. Fostering real achievement may also depend on expanding our definition of what achievement means. If we want all students to achieve—not just on tests but in their lives—trying to understand as best we can who they are and where they are coming from may be the best place to start.

NOTE

1. Erik H. Erikson, *Identity: Youth and Crisis* (New York: W. W. Norton, 1968).

CHAPTER ONE

Identity and Possibility

Adolescent Development and the Potential of Schools

MICHAEL NAKKULA

It's who I am, man. I can't change that. My family made me this way . . . my neighborhood made me this way. People around here [this school] always want me to change, but I can't change. I mean, I could, but I ain't gonna. I been this way all my life and I'm probly gonna keep bein' this way. This is how I am. They [teachers, counselors, and school administrators] should know that. My mother came in and said to you she don't know how I got this way. That's crazy. She knows I'm just like my father, my brothers, my uncles, and all these crazy people [kids in the neighborhood]. I gotta fight every day after school. How you gonna be any different when you gotta deal with that every day?

—*Mac, 14-year-old eighth grader*

Dealing with it every day—as Mac succinctly puts it—is precisely how and when identity develops. Contrary to popular misinterpretations of identity development theory, identity is not the culmination of a key event or series of events, although key events can play an important role in the larger process.[1] In fact, it is not the culmination of anything. It is, rather, the lived experience of an ongoing process—the process of integrating successes, failures, routines, habits, rituals, novelties, thrills, threats, violations, gratifications, and frustrations into a coherent and evolving interpretation of who we are. Identity is the embodiment of self-understanding. We are who we understand ourselves to be, as that understanding is shaped and lived out in everyday experience.

MAC: A MINI CASE STUDY

What is the "it" that/who Mac claims to be? "It's who I am, man. I can't change that." Mac shared this self-perception in a conversation I had with him following a suspension hearing. (I was his school counselor at the time.) The principal of the middle school Mac attended called his mother and me into his office to discuss potential consequences stemming from Mac's latest fight. As usual, Mac had beaten somebody up . . . well, had sort of beaten somebody up. He had not hurt the boy badly, had not used a weapon, and had not engaged in a prolonged battle that involved multiple participants on both sides of the conflict. (These latter actions come with consequences far more serious than those considered in a suspension hearing.) Rather, Mac had simply "taught the kid a lesson . . . not to mess with me . . . you don't call me a faggot and get away with it. . . . I pulled him in an empty classroom, threw him on the floor, and punched him in the face a few times." There was no "he started it" in Mac's conversation with the principal. He accepted full responsibility for his actions, refused to apologize, and was open to whatever punishment the principal deemed fair. As Mac explained, "It's his school. He has to do whatever he thinks is right. He should punish me . . . he has to. But that ain't gonna change what I have to do to take care of myself."

On the surface at least, the "it" Mac claims to be is a quick-triggered, self-protective fighter. If attacked, he strikes back instinctively, with just enough force to resolve the situation and preserve his integrity. From the outside, he might be defined as violent and homophobic. Those attributes might be seen as central to his identity. But Mac does not define himself by these terms. He views his fighting as a survival tactic within the contexts of a tough family, neighborhood, and school. Thus, Mac's "identity" as a fighter has been shaped by, and in his mind is consistent with, the environments in which he spends his time. Violence to him implies premeditation, maiming, and the use of weapons, things with which he does not associate himself. Fighting in response to an external threat, on the other hand, is seen as a noble act of self-defense. According to Mac, it is important to develop a tough reputation not for the sake of being cool, as many adults assume, but rather to be safe and respected in the environments he must navigate.

A bit more scratching beneath the surface uncovers a deeper understanding of the "who I am" Mac claims to be. Fighting under the circumstances in which he lives is one event within a coherent pattern of activity in his everyday interactions. Mac feels a compelling need and desire to be a stable, recognizable part of his environment. "Being known" in a particular way at school and in his neighborhood is important to him. He trusts his own instincts for self-protection, and he wants others to know how he will respond. "I trust myself" and "you can count on me" are two statements that apply equally well to Mac, and each seems equally important to him. He knows himself as a self-protective fighter, and others know him in this way. But he also knows himself as helpful and kind, as honest and stubborn, and others know him by these characteristics as well. He can be counted on. Teachers know this. The principal knows this. His family knows this. His friends know this. He can be counted on to fight and get into trouble, and he can be counted on to help family and friends in need. His word is solid.

This mini-portrait of Mac touches upon many of the themes critical to adolescent identity. It depicts the integration of a stable way of being; it raises questions about the implications of adolescent identity for later development; it points to the complexity of meaning that underlies seemingly straightforward interpretations of identity-related behaviors; and it exemplifies the multiple roles of context, including but not limited to school, in shaping identity. But the core theme of this chapter is that identity development occurs through the interactions among all of the activities and human relationships that take place within specific contexts.

Given the amount of time young people spend in school, the educational context plays a critical role in identity formation. Clearly, however, time spent within a setting has less impact on identity than does the nature of involvement. The activities and relationships most influential to identity development are those in which youth are most invested and through which they experience the deepest gratification and most meaningful reinforcement. Because the answer to the identity question "Who am I?" is inordinately shaped by the contexts, relationships, and activities in which youth are most deeply invested, it is essential that our schools be environments in which young people choose to invest and through which their investment is adequately reciprocated.

ERIKSON'S CLASSIC IDENTITY MODEL: IMPLICATIONS AND LIMITATIONS

When influential child and adolescent psychologist Erik Erikson was constructing his original notions of identity development in the 1940s and

1950s, the world was a very different place. Taking a personal stand to "be" a certain way was arguably easier in the immediate postwar United States, for example, than it is today. In 1950, when Erikson's groundbreaking work *Childhood and Society* was published, there was intense pride in "being an American." Individual identity could clearly be organized around national identity. Perhaps for the first time, and certainly with the most clarity, "American" was embraced as its own nationality, rather than being viewed solely as the melting pot of other nationalities. For adolescents of that era, figuring out what to be and how to be were clearly linked to "what kind of American to be" and "how to be a productive American."[2]

By 1968, when Erikson's second major work, *Identity: Youth and Crisis,* was published, it meant something very different to be an American.[3] Participation in and opposition to the Vietnam War had split the country's loyalties, and the civil rights, women's, and labor movements had raised the national consciousness about what it meant to be an American of a particular race, class, and gender. The largely unified, pro-American identity parameter of 1950 had split into crisis by 1968. It is little wonder, then, that "identity crisis" became a fundamental organizing principle of Erikson's later work and a focal point, in one form or another, of the many identity development models that followed.[4]

In Erikson's widely cited lifespan model of identity development, which begins in infancy, each stage ushers in a unique "crisis" or critical task to be negotiated.[5] Successful negotiation of the task creates a critical opportunity for positive ongoing development; unsuccessful negotiation results in progressively heightened challenges. For example, the crisis of infancy—which Erikson called "trust versus mistrust"—sets the foundation for all subsequent developmental challenges and opportunities.[6] The infant fortunate enough to approach toddlerhood with a basic sense of trust in her caretakers and surrounding environment is provided with a secure foundation from which to negotiate the next "crisis" of "autonomy versus shame and doubt."[7] The infant who has been mistreated or neglected, and as a result approaches toddlerhood with increased levels of fear and anxiety, is more likely to struggle in her early steps toward autonomy and in subsequent attempts at relational connectedness. In short, each life stage is marked by a developmental crisis that brings both risk and opportunity for future growth.[8]

By adolescence, enough experiences of success, failure, and sheer survival have accumulated that the magnitude of the developmental crisis is exponentially compounded. In addition, growth in cognitive development is such that the understanding of one's own situation makes the possibilities for the crisis still more complex. According to this model, adolescence provides the best last chance to rework some of the prior crises, and thus reset the course for positive subsequent development. Erikson's stance on adolescence can be criticized as either idealistically hopeful or fatalistically hopeless. Is it really possible to substantially rework the damages of childhood via a successful identity struggle in adolescence? And is it really the case that the unsuccessful negotiation of adolescent identity leaves one fated to a lifetime of confusion, failure, and despair? The great likelihood is that the truth lies somewhere in the middle. Still, few if any psychologists would argue that the process of identity development is not crucially important and deeply felt during adolescence, even if the repercussions may be less dramatic than Erikson depicted.

CRISIS AS OPPORTUNITY IN ADOLESCENCE

The risk of identity crisis in adolescence is accompanied by a unique opportunity for young people to interrupt the cycle of unhealthy development that may have evolved throughout childhood, according to Erikson's model. If adolescents can experience a "developmental moratorium," in which they have an opportunity to reflect on and experiment with who they are, particularly with respect to their skills, interests, and relationships with others, they are likely to move toward adulthood with enhanced possibilities for long-term health and success. In essence, such a moratorium provides a "break in the developmental action." It allows adolescents to use their advanced cognitive abilities to explore a range of possibilities for future development—to ask, "Given my present interests, aptitudes, and motivations, what life course(s) should I pursue?" Remaining open to possibility is the key to a successful moratorium experience.

The opposite of moratorium in Erikson's framework is "foreclosure." The foreclosed identity results from an adolescent making a commitment to a particular life course without adequately exploring alternatives. We hear the hints of such a foreclosure in Mac's opening statements:

> People around here [this school] always want me to change, but I can't change. I mean, I could, but I ain't gonna. I been this way all my life and I'm probly gonna keep bein' this way.

In many respects, Mac's statements reflect a deeper moratorium than Erikson had in mind, at least in his early writing. The classical notion of developmental moratorium focused on role clarification: figuring out what role to play in society in relationship to work and career. But Mac is referring to more than a role in the workplace; he is referencing a way of being: "I been this way all my life and I'm probly gonna keep bein' this way." There are tones of both resignation and personal ownership in Mac's comment. He sees himself as destined to fulfill a certain kind of role in society, based in part on his gender, social class, and family history, and this expectation seems to be a deeply embedded component of his identity.

CREATING POSSIBILITY

If Mac's teachers, counselors, or parents wanted to support him in exploring a different life course, what form would a moratorium take? For Mac, and for many other urban teens living in poor and working-class communities, concern over prematurely committing to a working role in society is largely irrelevant. A job, any job, is often viewed as an opportunity too good to pass up. Delaying work commitments to explore more gratifying long-term work-related options is simply unrealistic.

Still, adults who work with adolescents can increase their options for healthy development by presenting them with multiple opportunities to redirect their investment of mental or psychic energy. The psychologists Mihaly Csikszentmihalyi and Reed Larson have shown how development is very much a process of this kind of energy investment. They note that we grow most strongly in the areas in which we most thoroughly invest.[9] Mac has invested heavily in his prowess as a strong, successful fighter and defender of his word. It could be argued that his overinvestment in this area has left him with deficits to contend with in other areas. He has foreclosed on other options in order to support that which he knows best. His identity, from this perspective, will be overly determined by a narrow band of experience.

There is a strong movement afoot in psychology and related youth development disciplines to provide a broader range of developmental opportunities for young people. Rather than viewing Mac and others like him as deficient and in need of treatment, this emerging perspective views them as capable, but in need of a greater number of engaging opportunities. Consistent with this notion, youth development programs and broader community initiatives of all types are sprouting up across the country.[10] Although most of these "sprouts" never make it beyond the seedling stage, others grow and interact with schools to create viable opportunities for developmental experimentation. Rather than creating a space for adolescents to stop and reflect, these initiatives provide them with an opportunity to pivot and reinvest vital psychic energy. As noted previously, identity development happens every day and everywhere, but it develops most actively where energy is invested most thoroughly. In this regard, a program, an activity, or a hobby that calls for a deep investment of time and energy does more than build skills and interests in a particular area; deep investment builds into and upon the very sense of who we are.

Mentoring programs. This kind of youth development work has taken a wide variety of forms over the past two decades. Large organizations like Big Brothers Big Sisters have made an extraordinary contribution, not only by providing thousands of adolescents with opportunities for one-to-one mentoring but also by helping to raise our awareness of the value of adult-youth relationships both within and outside the family. For youth, meaningful exposure to future possibilities and possible ways of being tends to be facilitated by caring adults who can provide guidance and modeling.[11] School-based mentoring is becoming progressively more common as schools grapple with the reality that many young people have little access to caring adult role models.[12] A particular characteristic of many school-based mentoring approaches is the effort to incorporate academic learning into the mentoring relationship. This approach gives youth who are disconnected from school or who may view educational success as antithetical to their self-understanding the opportunity to connect with learning in a different way. Through relationships with their mentors, many such youth come to experience education as relevant to who they are and who they hope to become, often for the first time.

One-to-one mentoring and other relationally based youth development programs might be viewed as contemporary "holding environments," designed to provide youth with some semblance of a developmental moratorium.[13] They are not explicitly intended to help young people explore different career paths or adult roles in society, but they are designed as spaces for self-exploration and development. Such programs cannot and should not jolt young people out of the pressing demands of their everyday lives, but they often constitute an important space for adolescents to pause, connect with the world in a different way, and perhaps experience a change in life course, whether subtle or dramatic.

Sports and other activities. Over the past four years, my colleagues and I have been studying a girls' development program organized around rowing. G-Row (Girls Row) recruits between twenty and thirty middle and high school girls from Boston's public schools to participate in an intensive rowing program. Founded by Holly Metcalf, an Olympic rowing gold medalist, G-Row is explicitly designed to use the activity of rowing to help girls build strength, character, and a sense of self. In a variety of ways, this program epitomizes the role youth programming can have on development generally and identity development more specifically.

For starters, rowing is largely an elite sport, available primarily to young people privileged enough to encounter rowing opportunities in their private boarding schools or colleges. Its availability to urban girls has an immediate impact on the ways in which they encounter a culture quite different from their own. The girls place themselves in relation to rowers in the other boats, who are private school and college students. By placing themselves in meaningful relationship to these rowers, they have entered another world and expanded their own horizons in an important way. It is not that their home environment or community is deficient relative to this new context, but rather that their exposure to and exploration of the larger world has been expanded.

But the identity implications of participating in an elite sport against competitors from dramatically different environments is only a small part of G-Row's impact on participants' experience of themselves. The girls talk proudly about pushing through barriers in ways they could never have imagined, about calloused hands that mark the commitment to their sport, about opportunities they see for rowing in college, and, most important, about the profound implications of connecting deeply with their teammates and coaches. G-Row is about skill development in multiple arenas: rowing, building physical strength, mental focus and discipline, and teamwork. But the guiding center of these self-development tasks is relational connectedness. As one rower explained about her coach, "She's in my face . . . she's on my butt every day . . . she has my back and I never question that. I don't want to let her down in the race by not giving it everything I have."

Such comments are shared year after year in our interviews and focus groups as the girls talk about their teammates and coaches. G-Row is much less about the skills and excitement of rowing, or even about individual growth, than it is about relationship development. And relationship development is very much the anchor of identity. Identity from a relational perspective is not just a matter of how I see myself in relationship with and to others; more accurately, it is a matter of how I have come to see myself through the profound influences of meaningful relationships. While I am not arguing that youth development programs such as G-Row can compete with the influences of lifelong family relationships on identity development, I am claiming that such programs can serve to profoundly redirect the investment of vital psychic energy. This redirection, in turn, can set youth on a longer-term course of relational and skill-development experiences that become progressively more central to a core sense of self.

CONNECTEDNESS TO SCHOOL

While activities like mentoring and athletics provide special contexts for identity exploration, adolescents' everyday experiences of family, friends, and school arguably carry the most weight for ongoing identity development. For the vast majority of youth, school is the single context within which the combination of skill and relationship development occurs on a regular basis, day in and day out. Furthermore, the core educational mission of schooling has obvious implications for identity development. For example, students strong in specific academic subjects often integrate these talents into their identities as aspiring college students. But what do schools contribute to identity development beyond the basics of education, and how can they maximize this contribution on behalf of their students?

To reiterate a theme that runs throughout this chapter, schools that promote positive identity development are rich in engaging activities in which students can invest their psychic energy, and they value the role of relationships at all levels of learning. Good teachers teach their subject matter well; great teachers engage students in the learning tasks of the moment and instill in them the desire to keep learning long after graduation. Teachers who have this kind of impact do more than impart knowledge; they engage their students, they relate to them, and in turn they foster their students' relationship to learning. The act of engagement is the key to identity development in schools, as elsewhere. This act can occur in classrooms between teacher and pupil, in gymnasiums between coach and player, in hallways among friends, and in the guidance office between counselor and future college applicant. Engagement that has the greatest impact tends to be reciprocal.

It is not enough for teachers to move students, as this movement is unilateral or unidirectional. Transformational learning occurs when students sense that they too have moved their teachers—through their efforts and accomplishments and through their deep engagement in the learning process. Teaching and learning are a two-way street: When they work optimally, all parties are transformed. In the school counseling arena, Sharon Ravitch and I have called this process "reciprocal transformation," based on our repeated observation of the extent to which counselors are affected by the students they counsel.[14] In the athletic arena, examples of reciprocal transformation are readily apparent in the joyous victory celebrations and tearful expressions of defeat shared by coaches and players. Whatever the school-related context, adolescent identity will be profoundly influenced by those relationships in which it is clear to the student that she matters to the adult as much as the adult matters to her.

But what about Mac and students like him who are far more engaged in the street than in school? He is not particularly interested in sports, art, or music, much less math and reading. How can schools engage such students in order to make a meaningful contribution to their identity development?

Through a school-based project called Inventing the Future (Project IF), my colleagues and I reach out to educationally disengaged students in an effort to forge links between their present situations and future possibilities. We learned through the project that Mac wanted to be a fireman. Of all the students in his class he had perhaps the clearest vision of his potential career. We learned that he wanted to be a fireman because he wanted to save lives. Someone close to him had died in a fire when he was a child, and he was committed to saving others from a similar fate. Our project uncovered something about Mac that others in the school had not known. The public expression of his commitment to saving lives moved the adults and students who heard his story during our classroom activity, just as his telling it seemed to move him. Mac could no longer be narrowly defined by those present as a quick-tempered street fighter who had little interest in school. He held a different position in the class after that, and he played a different role.

In order to find what boils beneath the surface of students like Mac, schools must make explicit efforts to reach out and engage them beyond the basic curriculum. The curriculum represents the school's agenda. While it is critical that this agenda be met, it is similarly critical to meet the students where they are and to learn *their* agendas. Only by meeting the students where they stand now can we actively participate in the development of where they are going and who they are becoming.

NOTES

1. The most widely cited, and often misinterpreted, theory is Erik Erikson's lifespan model, which frames identity development as the hallmark of adolescence (see subsequent notes).
2. Erik H. Erikson, *Childhood and Society* (New York: W. W. Norton, 1950).
3. Erik H. Erikson, *Identity: Youth and Crisis* (New York: W. W. Norton, 1968).
4. William Cross, *Black Identity: Rediscovering the Distinction between Personal Identity and Reference Group Orientation* (New York: Africana Studies and Research Center, Cornell University, 1980); Jean Phinney, "Multiple Group Identities: Differentiation, Conflict, and Integration," in Jane Kroger (ed.), *Discussions on Ego Identity* (Hillsdale, NJ: Lawrence Erlbaum Associates, 1993), 47–74.
5. While identity theorists generally concur that adolescence marks a critical era in the life cycle when experiences from childhood are integrated into a revised understanding of who one is and where one fits within her social context, there is a great deal of debate over the actual nature of adolescent identity development. Erikson's model has been widely critiqued by feminist and relational psychologists such as Miller, Pastor, McCormick, and Fine, for example, as being largely representative of White, middle-class male development. Specifically, their claim is that the model overemphasizes autonomy, individualism, and personal freedom at the cost of relational and cultural connectedness. Although this type of critique questions the potential outcomes of identity development in the human life cycle, it does not contradict Erikson's argument that the "process" of identity development is often defined by engagement in a crisis of self-understanding or self-understanding in relationship to others. See Jean Baker Miller, *Toward a New Psychology of Women* (Boston: Beacon Press, 1976); Jennifer Pastor, Jennifer McCormick, and Michelle Fine, "Makin' Homes: An Urban Girl Thing," in Bonnie J. Ross Leadbeater and Niobe Way (eds.), *Urban Girls: Resisting Stereotypes, Creating Identities* (New York: New York University Press, 1996), 15–34.
6. Erikson, *Identity*, 96–107.
7. Erikson, *Identity*, 107–114.
8. Erikson, *Identity*.
9. Mihaly Csikszentmihalyi and Reed Larson, *Being Adolescent: Growth and Conflict in the Teenage Years* (New York: Basic Books, 1984).
10. Peter L. Benson and Karen J. Pittman (eds.), *Trends in Youth Development: Visions, Realities and Challenges* (Boston: Kluwer Academic Press, 2001); Martha R. Burt, Gary Resnick, and Emily Novick, *Building Supportive Communities for At-Risk Adolescents: It Takes More Than Services* (Washington, DC: American Psychological Association, 1998).
11. Jean Rhodes, *Stand by Me: The Risks and Rewards of Mentoring Today's Youth* (Cambridge, MA: Harvard University Press, 2002).
12. Carla Herrera, "School-Based Mentoring: A First Look into Its Potential," unpublished study, 1999.
13. The pediatrician and child psychiatrist D. W. Winnicott originally defined "holding environments" as safe and nurturing spaces for healthy child development. See

D. W. Winnicott, "Adolescent Immaturity," in D. W. Winnicott, *Home Is Where We Start From: Essays by a Psychoanalyst* (New York: W. W. Norton, 1990), 150–166.

14. Michael Nakkula and Sharon Ravitch, *Matters of Interpretation: Reciprocal Transformation in Therapeutic and Developmental Relationships with Youth* (San Francisco: Jossey-Bass, 1998).

CHAPTER TWO

"Joaqu´n's Dilemma"

Understanding the Link between
Racial Identity and School-Related Behaviors

PEDRO A. NOGUERA

When I am asked to speak or write about the relationship between racial identity and academic performance, I often tell the story of my eldest son, Joaqu´n. Joaqu´n did extremely well throughout most of his early schooling. He was an excellent athlete (participating in soccer, basketball, and wrestling), played piano and percussion, and did very well in his classes. My wife and I never heard any complaints about him. In fact, we heard nothing but praise about his behavior from teachers, who referred to him as "courteous," "respectful," and "a leader among his peers." Then suddenly, in the tenth grade, Joaqu´n's grades took a nosedive. He failed math and science, and for the first time he started getting into trouble at school. At home he was often angry and irritable for no apparent reason.

My wife and I were left asking ourselves, "What's going on with our son? What's behind this sudden change in behavior?" Despite my disappointment and growing frustration, I tried not to allow Joaqu´n's behavior to drive us apart. I started spending more time with him and started listening more intently to what he had to tell me about school and his friends. As I did, several things became clear to me. One was that all of the friends he had grown up with in our neighborhood in South Berkeley, California (one of the poorest areas of the city), were dropping out of school. These were mostly Black, working-class kids who didn't have a lot of support at home or at school and were experiencing academic failure. Even though Joaqu´n came from a middle-class home with two supportive parents, most of his reference group—that is, the students he was closest to and identified with—did not.

The other thing that was changing for Joaqu´n was his sense of how he had to present himself when he was out on the streets and in school. As he grew older, Joaqu´n felt the need to project the image of a tough and angry young Black man. He believed that in order to be respected he had to carry himself in a manner that was intimidating and even menacing. To behave differently—too nice, gentle, kind, or sincere—meant that he would be vulnerable and preyed upon. I learned that for Joaqu´n, part of his new persona also involved placing less value on academics and greater emphasis on being cool and hanging out with the right people.

By eleventh grade Joaqu´n gradually started working out of these behaviors, and by twelfth grade he seemed to snap out of his angry state. He became closer to his family, his grades improved, he rejoined the soccer team, he resumed playing the piano, and he even started producing music. As I reflected on the two years of anger and self-destructiveness that he went through, I came to the conclusion that Joaqu´n was trying desperately to figure out what it meant to be a young Black man. I realized that, like many Black male adolescents, Joaqu´n was trapped by stereotypes, and they were pulling him down. During this difficult period it was very hard for me to help him through this process of identity formation. While he was in the midst of it the only thing I could do was talk to him, listen to him, and try to let him know what it was like for me when I went through adolescence.

As a high school student, I had coped with the isolation that came from being one of the few students of color in my advanced classes by working extra hard to prove that I could do as well as or better than my White peers. However, outside of the classroom I also worked hard to prove to my less studious friends that I was cool, or "down," as we would say. For me this meant playing basketball, hanging out, fighting when necessary, and acting like "one of the guys." I felt forced to adopt a split personality: I behaved one way in class, another way with my friends, and yet another way at home.

THE EMERGING AWARENESS OF RACE

Adolescence is typically a period when young people become more detached from their parents and attempt to establish an independent identity. For racial minorities, adolescence is also a period when young people begin to solidify their understanding of their racial identities. For many, understanding the significance of race means recognizing that membership in a racial category requires certain social and political commitments. Adolescence is a difficult and painful period for most young people. For those struggling to figure out the meaning and significance of their racial identities, the experience can be even more difficult.

Awareness of race and the significance of racial difference often begins in early childhood. We know from psychological research that the development of racial identity is very context dependent, especially in the early years. Children who attend racially diverse schools or reside in racially diverse communities are much more likely to become aware of race at an earlier age than children in more homogeneous settings.[1] In the latter context, race is often not a defining issue, nor is it a primary basis for identity formation. When children see their race as the norm they are less likely to perceive characteristics associated with it (e.g., physical appearance) as markers of inferiority.

In contrast, children who grow up in more integrated settings become aware of physical differences fairly early. Interacting with children from other racial and ethnic backgrounds in a society that has historically treated race as a means of distinguishing groups and individuals often forces young people to develop racial identities early. However, prior to adolescence they still do not usually understand the political and social significance associated with differences in appearance. For young children, being a person with different skin color may be no more significant than being thin or heavy, tall or short. Differences in skin color, hair texture, and facial features are simply seen as being among the many differences that all children have. In environments where racist and ethnocentric behavior is common, children may learn fairly early that racist speech is hurtful.[2] They may know that calling someone a nigger is worse than calling them stupid, but they may not necessarily understand the meaning of such words or know *why* their use inflicts hurt on others.

Four years ago I was conducting research with colleagues at an elementary school in East Oakland. We were interested in understanding how the practice of separating children on the basis of language differences affected their social relationships and perceptions of students from other groups. As is true in many parts of California, East Oakland was experiencing a major demographic change, as large numbers of Mexican and Central American immigrants were moving into communities that had previously been predominantly African American. As is often the case, schools in East Oakland served as the place where children from these groups encountered one another, and at several of the high schools there had been a significant increase in interracial conflict.[3]

In the elementary school where we did our research, we found that most of the Black and Latino students had little interaction with each other. Although they attended the same school, the students had been placed in separate classes, ostensibly for the purpose of serving their language needs. From our interviews with students we learned that even very young children viewed peers from the other racial group with suspicion and animosity, even though they could not explain why. Interestingly, when we asked the students why they thought they had been placed in separate classrooms, most thought it was to prevent them from fighting. We also found that the younger Mexican students (between ages five and eight) saw themselves as White, and the Black students also referred to the Mexican students as White. However, as the children entered early adolescence (age nine or ten), the Mexican youth began to realize that they were not considered White outside of this setting, and they began to understand for the first time that being Mexican meant something very different from being White.

Depending on the context, it is not uncommon for minority children to express a desire to reject group membership based on skin color, especially during early adolescence. As they start to realize that in this society to be Black or Brown means to be seen as "less than"—whether it be less smart, less capable, or less attractive—they will often express a desire to be associated with the dominant and more powerful group. This tendency was evident among some of the younger Mexican students in our study. However, as they grew older, the political reality of life in East Oakland served to reinforce their understanding that they were definitely not White. As one student told us, "White kids go to nice schools with swimming pools and grass, not a ghetto school like we go to."

In adolescence, awareness of race and its implications for individual identity become even more salient. For many young men and women of color, racial identity development is affected by some of the same factors that influence individual identity development in general. According to Erik Erikson and other theorists of child development, as children enter adolescence they become extremely conscious of their peers and seek out acceptance from their reference group.[4] As they become increasingly aware of themselves as social beings, their perception of self tends to be highly dependent on acceptance and affirmation by others. For some adolescents, identification with and attachment to peer groups takes on so much importance that it can override other attachments to family, parents, and teachers.

For adolescents in racially integrated schools, racial and ethnic identity also frequently take on new significance with respect to friendship groups and dating. It is not uncommon in integrated settings for pre-adolescent children to interact and form friendships easily across racial boundaries—if their parents or other adults allow them to do so.[5] However, as young people enter adolescence, such transgressions of racial boundaries can become more problematic. As they become increasingly aware of the significance associated with group differences, they generally become more concerned with how their peers will react to their participation in interracial relationships and they may begin to self-segregate. As they get older, young people also become more aware of the politics associated with race. They become more cognizant of racial hierarchies and prejudice, even if they cannot articulate the political significance of race. They can feel its significance, but they often cannot explain what it all means.

For the past three years I have been working closely with fifteen racially integrated school districts in the Minority Student Achievement Network (MSAN). At the racially integrated high schools in MSAN, students often become much more aware that racial-group membership comes with certain political commitments and social expectations. In these schools, high-achieving students of color, like my son Joaquín, are sometimes unwilling to enroll in Advanced Placement courses or engage in activities that have traditionally been associated with White students because they fear becoming estranged from their friends. If they appear to engage in behavior that violates racial norms, they may be seen as rejecting membership in their racial group and run the risk of being regarded as race traitors. For this reason, I have urged the districts in MSAN not to rely upon student initiative to break down racial barriers but to put the onus on school leaders to take steps that will make this border crossing easier and more likely.[6]

THEORIES OF THE IDENTITY-ACHIEVEMENT CONNECTION

For educators, understanding the process through which young people come to see themselves as belonging to particular racial categories is important because it has tremendous bearing on the so-called achievement gap. Throughout the United States, schools are characterized by increasing racial segregation[7] and widespread racial disparities in academic achievement.[8] Blatant inequities in funding, quality, and organization are also characteristic of the U.S. educational system. Despite overwhelming evidence of a strong correlation between race and academic performance, there is considerable confusion among researchers about how and why such a correlation exists.

The scholars whose work has had the greatest influence on these issues are John Ogbu and Signithia Fordham, both of whom have argued that Black students from all socioeconomic backgrounds develop "oppositional identities" that lead them to view schooling as a form of forced assimilation to White cultural values.[9] Ogbu and Fordham argue that Black students and other "nonvoluntary minorities" (e.g., Chicanos, Puerto Ricans, Native Americans, and others whose groups have been dominated by White European culture) come to equate academic success with "acting White." For these researchers, such perceptions lead to the devaluation of academic pursuits and the adoption of self-defeating behaviors that inhibit possibilities for academic success. In this framework, the few students who aspire to achieve academically must pay a heavy price for success. Black students who perform at high levels may be ostracized by their peers as traitors and sellouts and may be forced to choose between maintaining ties with their peers or achieving success in school.[10] This would explain why middle-class minority students like Joaquín might underperform academically despite their social and economic advantages.

My own research challenges Ogbu and Fordham's "acting White" thesis. While carrying out research among high school students in Northern California, I discovered that some high-achieving minority students are ostracized by their peers, but others learn how to succeed in both worlds by adopting multiple identities (as I did). Still others actively and deliberately challenge racial stereotypes and seek to redefine their racial identities by showing that it is possible to do well in school and be proud of who they are.

Claude Steele's work on the effects of racial stereotypes on academic performance helps provide a compelling explanation for the identity-achievement paradox. Through his research on student attitudes toward testing, Steele (twin brother of the more conservative Shelby) has shown that students are highly susceptible to prevailing stereotypes related to intellectual ability.[11] According to Steele, when "stereotype threats" are operative, they lower the confidence of vulnerable students and negatively affect their performance on standardized tests. Steele writes, "Ironically, their susceptibility to this threat derives not from internal doubts about their ability but from their identification with the domain and the resulting concern they have about being stereotyped in it."[12] According to Steele, the debilitating effects of stereotypes can extend beyond particular episodes of testing and can have an effect on overall academic performance.

RACE IN THE SCHOOL CONTEXT

Stereotypes and Expectations

As Steele's research illustrates, in the United States we have deeply embedded stereotypes that connect racial identity to academic ability, and children become aware of these stereotypes as they grow up in the school context. Simply put, there are often strong assumptions made that if you're White you'll do better in school than if you're Black, or if you're Asian you'll do better in school than if you're Latino. These kinds of stereotypes affect both teachers' expectations of students and students' expectations of themselves.

One of the groups most affected by these stereotypes is Asian Americans. There is a perception in many schools that Asians are naturally academically gifted, especially in math. This stereotype is based on the following notions: 1) that Asians are inherently smart (either for genetic or cultural reasons); 2) that they have a strong work ethic; 3) that they are passive and deferential toward authority; and 4) that unlike other minorities, they don't complain about discrimination. These perceptions make up what is often called the model minority stereotype. (See "Model Minorities and Perpetual Foreigners" by Stacey J. Lee, pp. 41–49.)

One of my former students, Julian Ledesma, now a researcher in the Office of the President of the University of California, has been doing research on the model minority stereotype at a high school in Oakland. He started his work by interviewing various teachers and students about who they believed were "the smartest kids." In nearly every case, those he asked reported that the Asians were the smartest students. Even Asian students who were doing poorly in school reported that Asians were the smartest. The surprising thing about their responses to this question was that the average grade point average for Asians at the school was 1.8.

One reason for the gross misconception at this school was that Asians were overrepresented in the honors courses and were among the students with the highest ranks in their class. Yet these successful students were not representative of Asians as a whole at the school. Overall, Asian students were dropping out in high numbers and not doing well academically. The school where Julian did his research also had a considerable gang problem among Asians. Yet, because the stereotype is so powerful, students and teachers at the school were more likely to regard the majority of Asian students as the exceptions and the smaller numbers who were successful as the norm.

The stereotypical images we hold of certain groups are powerful in influencing what people see and expect of students. Unless educators consciously try to undermine and work against these kinds of stereotypes, they often act on them unconsciously. Our assumptions related to race are so deeply entrenched that it is virtually impossible for us not to hold them unless we take conscious and deliberate action. (See the commentary by Beverly Daniel Tatum, "Opening the Dialogue about Race at School," pp. 36–39.)

Sorting Practices and "Normal" Racial Separation

Beyond these stereotypes, the sorting practices that go on in schools also send important messages to students about the meaning of racial categories. For example, in many schools students in the remedial classes are disproportionately Black and Brown, and students often draw conclusions about the relationship between race and academic ability based on these patterns. They might say to themselves, "Well, I guess the kids in these 'slow' classes are not as smart as those in the honors classes." They also notice that the students who are most likely to be punished, suspended, and expelled are the darker students.

In addition to reinforcing stereotypes, grouping practices, which teachers and administrators often say are not based on race but on ability or behavior, often have the effect of reinforcing racial separation. Unless the adults in a school are conscious of how this separation influences their own perceptions and those of students, over time this separation may be regarded as normal. For example, Black students may assume that, because there are no Black students in advanced or honors courses, they cannot excel academically. Of course, Black students can distinguish themselves in sports, because there are numerous examples of Black individuals who do. Similarly, White students may assume that they should not seek academic assistance from tutorial programs, especially if those programs primarily serve Black or Brown students. When these kinds of norms associated with race take on a static and determining quality, they can be very difficult to counteract.

Students who receive a lot of support and encouragement at home may be more likely to cross over and work against these separations. But, as my wife and I found for a time with Joaquín, middle-class African American parents who try to encourage their kids to excel in school often find this can't be done because the peer pressure against crossing these boundaries is too great.

The racial separation we see in schools might also be considered an element of the "hidden curriculum," an unspoken set of rules that "teaches" certain students what they can and cannot do because of who they are. There are aspects of this hidden curriculum that are not being taught by the adults; students are teaching it to each other. No adult goes onto the playground and says, "I don't want the boys and girls to play together." The girls and boys do that themselves, and it's a rare child who crosses over. Why? Because those who violate gender norms are often ostracized by their peers. The girls who play with the boys become known as tomboys, and the boys who play with the girls become known as sissies. Although the children are sanctioning each other without instruction from adults, they are engaging in behavior that has been learned from adults—not explicitly, but implicitly. Adults can reinforce narrow gender roles by promoting certain activities, such as highly physical sports for boys and dance for girls.

In many schools there may not be explicit messages about race, but students receive implicit messages about race all the time that inform what they think it means to be a member of a particular racial group. For example, children receive messages about beauty standards. Who are the favored students and what are their characteristics? Who are the people who get into trouble a lot and what are *their* characteristics? Much of the time preferential (or nonpreferential) treatment is very much related to race. In addition, when students see Black students overrepresented on the basketball team but underrepresented in Advanced Placement courses, or Latino students overrepresented among those who've gotten into trouble but underrepresented among those receiving awards, they get a clear sense about the meaning of race. The hidden curriculum related to race presents racial patterns as normal and effectively reinforces racial stereotypes. When it is operative it can completely undermine efforts to raise student achievement because students may believe that altering racial patterns simply is not possible.

Too often educators assume that, because of the choices Black students make about such things as whom to socialize with or which classes to take, they are anti-intellectual.[13] However, the vast majority of Black students I meet express a strong desire to do well in school. The younger students don't arrive at school with an anti-intellectual orientation. To the degree that such an orientation develops, it develops *in* school, and from their seeing these patterns and racial hierarchies as permanent. Because a great deal of this behavior plays out in schools, educators can do something about it.

WHAT *CAN* EDUCATORS DO?

Understanding and debunking racial stereotypes, breaking down racial separations, and challenging the hidden curriculum are tasks not just for teachers, but for principals, administrators, and entire school communities. In addition, there are a number of things educators can do to support their students' positive racial identity development.

First, educators can make sure that students are not segregating themselves by sitting in racially defined groups in the classroom. For teachers, this can be as simple as mixing students and assigning them seats. Or, if work groups are created, students can be assigned to groups in ways that ensure that students of different backgrounds have an opportunity to work together. This approach to race mixing is often far more effective than holding an abstract conversation about tolerance or diversity. By working together, students are more likely to form friendships naturally, and as they gain familiarity with one another they may be more willing to break racial norms. If teachers let students choose, they will more than likely choose those they perceive to be "their own kind."

Second, educators can encourage students to pursue things that are not traditionally associated with members of their group. If students of color are encouraged by adults to join the debating team or the science club, to play music in the band, or to enroll in advanced courses, it will be possible for greater numbers to challenge racial norms. Extracurricular activities in particular can serve a very important role in this regard and give young people a chance to get to know each other in situations that are not racially loaded. As is true for work groups, in the course of playing soccer or writing for the newspaper, students can become friends. Research on extracurricular activities has shown that sports, music, theater, and other activities can play an important role in building connections among young people and breaking down the very insidious links between racial identity and academic achievement.[14]

Third, teachers can find ways to incorporate information related to the history and culture of students into the curriculum. This is important in helping students understand what it means to be who they are, an essential aspect of the identity formation process for adolescents. Literature also can be very effective in this regard because it can help students to identify and empathize with people from different backgrounds. Field trips and out-of-class experiences that provide students with opportunities to learn about the experiences of others can also help expand their horizons.

Finally, an effective teacher who is able to inspire students by getting to know them can actually do a great deal to overcome anti-academic tendencies. They can do this by getting students to believe in themselves, by getting them to learn how to work hard and persist, and by getting them to dream, plan for the future, and set goals. When you talk to students who have been successful, they speak over and over again about the role that significant adults have played at various points in their lives.[15] They talk about how these adults helped them recognize their own potential, and how they opened doors that the students previously did not know existed.

I believe there are many young people who are crying out for supportive relationships with caring adults. Differences in race, gender, or sexual orientation need not limit a teacher's ability to make a connection with a young person. In my own work with students and schools I have generally found kids to be the least prejudiced of all people. They tend to respond well to caring adults regardless of what they look like. However, they can also tell if the adults who work with them are sincere or are acting out of guilt and faked concern.

Today, most social scientists recognize race as a social rather than a biological construct. It is seen as a political category created largely for the purpose of justifying exploitation and oppression.[16] For many adults and kids, especially those of mixed heritage, the categories often do not even correspond to who they think they are. Rather than being a source of strength, the acquisition of racial identities may be a tremendous burden.

For many years to come, race will undoubtedly continue to be a significant source of demarcation within the U.S. population. For many of us it will continue to shape where we live, pray, go to school, and socialize. We cannot simply wish away the existence of race or racism, but we can take steps to lessen the ways in which the categories trap and confine us. As educators who should be committed to helping young people realize their intellectual potential as they make their way toward adulthood, we have a responsibility to help them find ways to expand their notions of identity related to race and, in so doing, help them discover all that they may become.

NOTES

1. Beverly Daniel Tatum, "Talking about Race, Learning about Racism: The Application of Racial Identity Development Theory in the Classroom," *Harvard Educational Review* 62, no. 1 (1992): 1–24; William E. Cross, *Shades of Black: Diversity in African American Identity* (Philadelphia: Temple University Press, 1991); Jean S. Phinney, "Ethnic Identity in Adolescents and Adults: Review of Research," *Psychological Bulletin* 108, no. 3 (1991): 499–514.
2. Barry Troyna and Bruce Carrington, *Education, Racism and Reform* (London: Routledge, 1990).
3. Pedro Noguera and Miranda Bliss, *A Four-Year Evaluation Study of Youth Together* (Oakland, CA: Arts, Resources and Curriculum, 2001).
4. Erik H. Erikson, *Identity: Youth and Crisis* (New York: W. W. Norton, 1968).

5. Troyna and Carrington, *Education, Racism and Reform.*

6. Pedro Noguera, "The Role of Social Capital in the Transformation of Urban Schools," in Susan Saegert, J. Philip Thompson, and Mark R. Warren (eds.), *Social Capital and Poor Communities* (New York: Russell Sage Foundation, 2001).

7. Gary Orfield and Susan Eaton, *Dismantling Desegregation* (New York: New Press, 1996).

8. Belinda Williams, "Closing the Achievement Gap," in Milli Pierce and Deborah L. Stapleton (eds.), *The 21st-Century Principal: Current Issues in Leadership and Policy* (Cambridge, MA: Harvard Education Press, 2003); Pedro Noguera and Antwi Akom, "Disparities Demystified," *The Nation*, June 5, 2000.

9. John Ogbu, "Opportunity Structure, Cultural Boundaries, and Literacy," in Judith A. Langer (ed.), *Language, Literacy, and Culture: Issues of Society and Schooling* (Norwood, NJ: Ablex Press, 1987); Signithia Fordham, *Blacked Out: Dilemmas of Race, Identity, and Success at Capital High* (Chicago: University of Chicago Press, 1996); Signithia Fordham and John Ogbu, "Black Students and School Success: Coping with the Burden of Acting White," *Urban Review* 18 (1986): 176–206.

10. Other researchers, such as Marcelo Suárez-Orozco of Harvard, have argued that recent immigrant students of color are largely immune to the insidious association between race and achievement that traps students from domestic minority backgrounds. For so-called voluntary minorities (Mexican, Asian, African, or West Indian), schooling is more likely to be perceived as a pathway to social mobility, and for this reason they are also more likely to adopt behaviors that increase the likelihood of academic success.

11. Claude Steele, "A Threat in the Air: How Stereotypes Shape the Intellectual Identities and Performance of Women and African Americans," *American Psychologist* 52 (June 1997): 613–629.

12. Steele, "A Threat in the Air," 614.

13. John H. McWhorter, *Losing the Race: Self-Sabotage in Black America* (New York: New Press, 2000); Deborah Meier, *The Power of Their Ideas: Lessons for America from a Small School in Harlem* (Boston: Beacon Press, 1995).

14. Laurence Steinberg, *Beyond the Classroom: Why School Reform Has Failed and What Parents Need to Do* (New York: Simon & Schuster, 1996).

15. Patricia Phelan, Ann Locke Davidson, Hanh Cao Yu, *Adolescents' Worlds: Negotiating Family, Peers, and School* (New York: Teachers College Press, 1997); James M. McPartland and Saundra M. Nettles, "Using Community Adults as Advocates or Mentors for At-Risk Middle School Students: A Two-Year Evaluation of Project RAISE," *American Journal of Education* 99, no. 4 (August 1991): 568–586.

16. Michael Omi and Howard Winant, *Racial Formation in the United States* (New York: Routledge, 1986); Reginald Horseman, *Race and Manifest Destiny* (Cambridge, MA: Harvard University Press, 1981).

Profile

Listening to Minority Students: One District's Approach to Closing the Achievement Gap

THOMAS FOWLER-FINN

> When we were presented the information describing the minority student achievement gap, we felt that we were stereotyped. We felt less human.
> —*High school senior, Fort Wayne (Ind.) Community Schools*

This young woman was one of a large group of African American and other minority students learning for the first time that students of color and lower-income students perform at dramatically lower levels than their peers by a variety of measures: state standardized tests, college entrance exams, grades, attendance and graduation rates, and others. The news that such a wide achievement gap exists hit hard at their identities. For some, the feelings of being "stereotyped" and "less human" led to anger, discouragement, and an undermining of self-confidence. For others more resilient, these feelings ignited determination and action.

As part of an ongoing effort to close the achievement gap between White students and students of color in the Fort Wayne Community Schools, minority students are participating in workshops with me (the superintendent) and with other district staff in which they reveal their personal perspectives and commit to leading projects in school and the community.* This past year in particular, through several days of discussion with African American and Latino high school students, we learned important lessons from these young people. We learned who they feel they are, how they see themselves in the school environment, and how their self-perceptions are bound up in

---

*Other aspects of the district's concerted effort to improve minority students' achievement and connection to school have included student surveys, staff development, mentoring programs for incoming freshmen, and an analysis of discipline referrals at district schools.

their academic achievement. The following is a snapshot of some of these lessons.

COMPLEX MOTIVATIONS

Roderick Sleet, an African American high school senior at the time he participated in our project (later an engineering student at Tennessee State), viewed himself as a streetwise kid who did well in school due to strong family support, but he worried about his friends. Rod felt that he and his African American peers were often not treated respectfully by teachers and feared that some of his peers would be tempted to seek the most expedient routes to short-term gratification. Rod was resilient, however, taking as a challenge events and issues that might have discouraged others. When he was a junior he entered an Advanced Placement class, and the teacher looked up at him and asked, "Are you sure you're in the right class?" He became determined to be an outstanding student to prove his worth to himself as well as to this teacher. But Rod felt that many teachers do not encourage students of color to see the value in learning and worried that, without such encouragement, his friends might not make it:

> When asked, "Why do we need to learn this?" teachers should not tell their students that it is to get a good job and earn a lot of money. I'm an urban kid, and as soon as you find other ways to earn money in the city, school is out the door. I absolutely hate it when a teacher says that, because I know if the wrong person hears that then they're going to say, "If the only reason to come to school is to earn money, I can find money other places and get it faster, so what's school for?" Tell students that the reason to go to school is to please themselves. Most teachers think that [telling kids about jobs and money] is a motivator, but it is a downplayer because it is making school secondary to money. And it isn't like that. You should get educated for yourself.

Rod's comments illustrate how educators' assumptions about minority students (in this case, that they are only interested in making money) can send a message that we think very little of them as human beings. These kinds of assumptions also fail to take into account the wide range of factors that motivate these students in school. The students we heard from in our workshops based their definitions of success on their own conduct, current performance versus past performance, the respect and recognition they received from others, how well they met obligations, and how they were doing in relation to family members and friends. Their identities are connected to all these factors, and for some they are also connected to their religion or the strong sense of a higher power. All of these things can serve as motivators. If we assume that the only thing an urban minority teen wants out of life is a financial payoff, we may close off an opportunity to inspire them to learn.

DIFFERENT VIEWS OF SUCCESS

Regardless of the mixed grades earned by the group of students we spoke with (some were A and B students, while others earned mostly Cs, Ds, and Fs), we found that all but a few students saw themselves as successful. Still, we noted differences in the ways the higher- and lower-achieving students viewed their success. Students who earned As and Bs connected their success to classwork and saw connections between good school performance and future plans and goals. For students with lower grades, these connections were much less clear. One student said, "I don't get straight Fs, so I think I'm a little successful." Another student equated success, in part, to "not getting into trouble," and one felt successful because "I am happy [about] where I am at in life." These lower-achieving students also were far more likely to point to class size, the presence of "troublemakers" in their classes, poor teachers, and other factors as obstacles to their success. Unlike their higher-achieving peers, they have not connected success in school with their own agency, nor have they internalized the ramifications of grades and standardized tests on their future aspirations. The markers these students use as criteria for success are therefore not consistent with the results-oriented focus currently being demanded of students and educators in the name of higher standards all over the country.

Although the self-acceptance of these lower-achieving students is heartening on one level, it is also cause for concern. Today, simply graduating from high school, even though you may be the first in your family to do so, is inadequate and will ensure a future with fewer options and closed doors. Educators in the Fort Wayne schools have been able to convince a large number of students and their families that dropping out is an unacceptable option (dropout rates for minority students have declined about 75 percent in the past decade or so), but there is much more work ahead. Our next task is to convince our staff of the need for higher expectations, not only because it will change the way we teach but also because it will communicate to students that their plans for the future can be based upon a higher level of attainment.

FROM ALIENATION TO COMMUNITY

> This workshop really did a lot for me and helped me understand what I must do to achieve my goals. It helped me to express the way I feel about our society and to know that I am not alone [in] the way I see people and things.
>
> *—Minority achievement workshop participant*

The minority students we have spoken with want very much to be a part of school life but have trepidation about getting connected. Many have told us, both in the workshops and in student school climate surveys we've conducted, that they have experienced too many rejections and too much subtle disrespect from teachers, administrators, staff, and their fellow students. The student whose comment is excerpted above also reveals that many minority students see themselves as alone in the struggle.

This is not to say that the students do not wish to see themselves as part of the larger community; in fact, they yearn for such connection. The students we spoke with wanted to be active members of the school as contributors and valued citizens. As our workshop participants indicated in their final reflections:

> I've learned that I can improve myself as a student and as a person by working with others to improve the minority student gap.

> Since last year's meeting, I have learned that I need to be more committed to the growth and development of others.

> I've learned that helping others brings joy and improvement to others and myself.

> This is an experience that I will remember. I plan to take all that I have learned and make an effort to change things at my school.

In addition to wanting to make a contribution to the school community, many students were motivated to close the achievement gap, in the words of one, "because it [the gap] makes me as an African American look bad." The data on the performance of minority students served as an awakening that drew very strong reactions, including some defensiveness. It hurt many to hear about the gap because it attacked their self-esteem; some felt threatened by it because it seemed to confirm societal messages they receive through personal experience with discrimination.

The plans students outlined to close the gap included roles for teachers, other minority students, and—as some participants noted pointedly—majority students. After all, they argued, there were plenty of White students with poor grades, too. Moreover, the participants reasoned that we *all* need to take responsibility for the entire learning community.

One of the greatest challenges facing school systems and teachers today is giving state standards and testing requirements meaning on a personal level for urban minority students. This is an enormous task, because it demands that we understand our students better. The perspectives and self-perceptions of high school students are key contributors to their academic achievement. Without a better understanding of the thoughts and feelings of our students and a school culture informed by and responsive to their perspectives, the most skilled teaching of an aligned, accountability-based curriculum will fall far short of student achievement goals. Closing the achievement gap is as dependent on closing "perception gaps," "caring gaps," and "culture gaps" as it is on any other factors. If we are prepared to listen, minority students can teach educators a lot about these gaps and how to close them.

Commentary

Opening the Dialogue about Race at School

BEVERLY DANIEL TATUM

Psychologist Beverly Daniel Tatum, president of Spelman College and the author of Why Are All the Black Kids Sitting Together in the Cafeteria? *and several other titles, has worked with schools for many years on developing ways to support the positive identity development of students of color. The first step in any such effort, Tatum says, is to open the dialogue about race and racism among teachers, school leaders, and other members of the community. In the following commentary, based on an interview, Tatum offers suggestions on how to begin this difficult and often painful conversation.*

WHY TALK ABOUT RACE?

In my presentations to students and educators, I often ask participants to think about an early race-related memory. I ask them to remember how old they were at the time the incident occurred and what feelings were associated with it. Everyone raises a hand; they all can think of something. Most people report an incident that happened during their childhood, perhaps as young as age three, but usually somewhere around five, six, or seven, in the early elementary years. In talking about the feelings associated with these memories, people often report emotions such as fear, embarrassment, anger, disappointment, and humiliation. Strong words come out. Then I ask, "Did you discuss it with anyone?" Very few people say that they did.

When young children are upset they usually talk about their experiences, so it is somewhat puzzling that a person would have an experience that she or he remembers years later, one with a negative emotion attached to it, yet not discuss it. When I ask why they didn't tell anyone, participants often respond by saying something like, "Maybe I tried to, but I was silenced" or "I had already picked up that I wasn't supposed to talk about it."

Most of us have had experiences that have been shaped in some way by racism, yet there's not much dialogue about it. In fact, there seems to be active socialization encouraging us *not* to talk about it. We use a lot of energy not talking about it, energy that would be better used interrupting it. A long time ago, James Baldwin wrote that not every problem that's recognized can be solved, but you can't solve a problem until it's recognized. If we acknowledge that we need to address issues of race and racism in order to support the positive identity development of students of color, first we have to be able to talk about them.

BEGINNING THE CONVERSATION

Opening the dialogue about race at school begins with creating a safe climate for discussion. People are not going to take the kind of psychological risks they need to take to explore these issues deeply unless they feel a sense of safety and confidentiality. People need to know that "we're all in this together, learning." They need to know that no one is blaming anyone else. It's all about working together to interrupt a system that was in place long before any of us showed up on the planet. It's not our fault, but we all have responsibilities.

A good place to start the dialogue is with colleagues who are interested. Sometimes people want to start with mandatory professional development training, and that is not necessarily a bad idea. It's great to send a clear message that this discussion is something that the leaders of the institution or the school district are supportive of and think is important. At the beginning, however, there are usually people whose life experiences or work with particular students have inspired them to think about these issues. If you start with these people, you can help them become fluent in their ability to talk about the issues in ways that engage others.

When I advocate this approach, some people say, "You're just preaching to the choir." That may be true, but I always reply that the choir needs rehearsal. When you work with the choir and they sing really well, other people are inspired to join them. If you start with the hard-core folks, those who really don't want to talk about the problem, don't want to think about it, and will do whatever they can to prevent you from doing so, you probably won't get very far.

Sometimes students are eager to address issues of race—and you might have a program for them as well. But if you don't also have a program for faculty, the students may get ahead of the faculty in terms of their comfort level and willingness to engage in the conversation. When that happens, faculty who haven't thought enough about these issues may shut down the conversation in ways that are very frustrating for the students.

OVERCOMING THE OBSTACLES

One of the challenges to talking about race in school is that most schools have a largely White teaching population. A lot of people will shut down around the topic because they feel as though they're going to be blamed, made to feel guilty, attacked, or otherwise maligned. There can be a lot of discomfort generated by these conversations. People struggle with language. What words can we use? The pressure to feel politically correct can be a part of it. There might be adults, parents as well as staff members, who think this conversation is inappropriate.

Sometimes people think that by talking about race they will create a problem where there is none. Someone will say something like, "Race relations have been very harmonious here. Why stir that pot?" Sometimes you hear this from parents of color, particularly in mostly White environments where there are few children of color. You might have a parent who will say, "My child is fine. She's doing fine. She has friends. She's getting along. I don't want you to rock that boat." They may think that to talk about these issues will generate discomfort for the student where it doesn't currently exist. In those situations, there may be more discomfort than the parent knows. The child doesn't necessarily have to be called names or be treated in a hostile way, but just the fact of being in a token position can be very uncomfortable for that child. Trying to figure out how to support a child's positive identity development under those circumstances is something that a parent may not have experience doing.

Sometimes teachers or school leaders will decide to open a school dialogue about race because there's been a very public problem, such as student protests or racist language written in the school newspaper. An incident has occurred, and the principal responds by saying, "We need to have this conversation." One of the dangers to this kind of reactive response is that there's a risk of not sustaining it long enough. The prevailing attitude might be, "We needed to respond, we responded, and now we don't have to talk about it anymore."

There is always the risk of discomfort when raising these issues, but one of the things you learn from doing it is that the discomfort often starts to subside. Sometimes what seems like fear can change to excitement. "You mean everyone can *talk about* that elephant in the room?" Once people are able to talk about what they've known was there all along, it's such a relief that it feels energizing. When you get to a point in the conversation where people start to feel the benefits of it, it's extremely powerful.

Unfortunately, what often happens instead is that people stop the dialogue before they get to that point. I sometimes use the analogy of treating an ear infection. When your child has an ear infection, you go to the doctor, they give you a two-week dose of antibiotics, and they tell you to give it to the child until it's gone. After a few days it seems that the ear infection has subsided—the child feels fine. She doesn't like the taste of the medicine and it's not very pleasant to keep administering it for fourteen days, but if you don't the bacteria that are being contained by the medicine won't be completely killed off. If you stop three or four days into treating the infection, maybe you've wounded it, but it will come back—and when it comes back, it comes back stronger.

Schools that have a race-related incident often want to respond to it. This response may make things a little bit better for a short period of time, but in that process you might also generate some long-term problems unless you give people the tools to work through it, process it, and start thinking about action strategies so that they feel they can *do* something about it. If you don't do those things, sooner or later there will be a new incident, just like there will be another ear infection.

At that point, not only is there a problem, but people don't want to go to another workshop. It's important to tell people right up front that this work is going to be hard, but it does get easier. If you can push through the discomfort, sustain yourself, and get to the next level, you can start to make meaningful progress.

CHAPTER THREE

Model Minorities and Perpetual Foreigners

The Impact of Stereotyping on Asian American Students

STACEY J. LEE

> The [Whites] will have stereotypes, like we're smart, . . . and sometimes
> you tend to be what they expect you to be and you just lose your identity
> . . . lose being yourself.
>
> —*High-achieving Asian American high school student*

Like other people of color in the United States, Asian Americans live under
the burden of racial stereotypes that structure their experiences and identities. Stereotypical images of Asian Americans include those of the valedictorian, the violin prodigy, the computer science whiz, the martial arts expert,
the greedy merchant, the gang member, and the bad driver. However, the
two most powerful and persistent stereotypes of Asian Americans are those
of the foreigner and the model minority.

The foreigner stereotype casts Asian Americans as perpetual foreigners
regardless of the length of time they or their families have been in the United
States.[1] The model minority stereotype depicts them as an exceedingly hardworking and successful group that has achieved the American Dream and
no longer experiences any barriers to success.[2] These two stereotypes have
been prevalent since the 1960s, and many of the current stereotypical beliefs
about Asian Americans are variations on these two recurrent themes. For

example, the valedictorian and violin prodigy are specific expressions of the model minority stereotype, and the gang member and bad driver are based on society's image of Asian Americans as perpetual foreigners.

As microcosms of American society, schools are places where the foreigner and model minority stereotypes are, unfortunately, alive and well among students and educators. As illustrated by numerous studies I have conducted with Asian American youth, these stereotypes can have a tremendous impact on these adolescents' self-concept, academic choices, and relationships with others in the school environment.[3]

THE PERPETUAL FOREIGNER STEREOTYPE
IN SOCIETY AND IN SCHOOLS

The image of the perpetual foreigner is perhaps the oldest stereotype of Asian Americans. While European American ethnics are accepted as "real" Americans soon after their arrival in the United States, Asian Americans are often viewed as outsiders.[4] Third-, fourth-, and even fifth-generation Asian Americans find that they are not seen as authentic Americans.[5] As Mia Tuan, a sociologist at the University of Oregon, explains in her book, *Forever Foreigners or Honorary Whites? The Asian Ethnic Experience Today*, "While white ethnics must actively assert their ethnic uniqueness if they wish this to feature prominently in their interactions with others, Asian ethnics are assumed to be foreign unless proven otherwise."[6]

To the extent that schools mirror the larger society, Asian American students are strongly affected by the perpetual foreigner stereotype. The Eurocentric curriculum that pervades most schools reinforces this stereotype through its silence around Asian American history.[7] Moreover, when the history or the literature of Asian Americans is taught in schools, it is usually relegated to the periphery of the curriculum, thereby marking Asian American issues as being somehow distinct from "mainstream American" concerns. Superficial approaches to multicultural education, such as programs that focus on Asian holidays and foods, represent another attempt to include Asian American issues in school curriculum, but the token approach with which many are implemented often serves merely to perpetuate the foreigner stereotype.

The image of Asian Americans as perpetual foreigners also informs the way many teachers view their Asian American students. In my research, I have found that teachers typically refer to students of Asian descent as "Asian" and not as "Asian American" or "American."[8] Although teachers may not intentionally be excluding Asian Americans from the category American, their language reveals an implicit assumption that the categories Asian and American are mutually exclusive. Also, the foreigner stereotype influences teachers' expectations of Asian American students as learners. For example, some teachers automatically assume that Asian American students will do better in math and science than in classes that require strong verbal skills. Other research suggests that some teachers equate accents (i.e., sounding foreign) with low cognitive abilities.[9]

In addition, the foreigner stereotype informs the way non–Asian American students view their Asian American peers. During moments of interracial conflict between students, this stereotype can emerge in full force, such as when non–Asian American students tell Asian American youth to "go back to where they came from" or use fake Asian accents to mock them.[10] Through this kind of behavior, non–Asian American youth send their peers a clear message: they are outsiders in their own schools.

INTERNALIZING—AND RESISTING—THE PERPETUAL FOREIGNER STEREOTYPE

Given the tremendous power of the perpetual foreigner stereotype in schools and society, many Asian American youth have internalized the belief that they are not real Americans. In fact, research suggests that many Asian American students view White people as the only real or authentic Americans.[11] A consistent finding in my studies has been that Asian American students reserve the term *American* for Whites and refer to all other groups by their specific races. When asked to describe an American, for example, many Asian American youth will describe a blond-haired, blue-eyed person.[12] Even Asian American students born in the United States are reluctant to use the term *American* to describe themselves because they know that others do not see them that way.[13]

Along with the belief that they are in some way foreign, many Asian American youth also have internalized the notion that this foreignness makes them inferior to real (i.e., White) Americans. These students hate qualities they understand to be associated with Asianness (i.e., foreignness). In an effort to distance themselves from these stigmatized images, some Asian American youth may reject things that they understand are perceived to be foreign, such as their names or languages. One Asian American student attending a large high school in the Northeast, for example, explained that he changed his name to an "American" one because he was tired of people making a joke of his name. "People make rhymes like 'fee fi fo fum,'" he explained. "I hate it."[14] Unfortunately, this student has learned that he cannot keep his Asian name and be accepted as American. He and other Asian Americans are forced to reject central aspects of their identities because Asianness and Americanness are seen as mutually exclusive.

Asian American students also have been found to go to great lengths to downplay physical traits that are associated with being Asian. Some girls and young women, for example, wear green or blue contact lenses in order to mask their Asianness and to emulate what they believe are White, "American" standards of beauty. One student explained that popular culture had influenced her ideas about beauty standards. She said, "Watching MTV affected the way I acted very much. I think I wanted to be more Americanized. I changed my hair color. I got colored contact lenses."[15]

In addition to self-perceptions, the foreigner stereotype also affects relationships among Asian American students themselves. In an effort to distance themselves from the stigma of foreignness, some U.S.-born Asian youth reject their non–U.S.-born peers, calling them such derogatory terms as *fobs* or *fobbies* (from the initials F.O.B. for "fresh off the boat") or mocking them for not being Americanized. One U.S.-born student at a high school in the Midwest expressed this disdain as follows: "Fobs don't care about clothes. . . . They dress in out-of-date 1980s-style clothes."[16] This student went on to explain that U.S.-born students were "into clothes and cars." By asserting the difference between themselves and non–U.S.-born youth, the American-born students are attempting to claim their rightful status as Americans, but they are unfortunately also reflecting their internalization of racist stereotypes.

The stigma associated with the foreigner stereotype also affects students' participation in classes. Students with Asian accents are often afraid to speak in class for fear that their non-Asian peers will mock the way they talk. Even Asian American students who speak accent-free English are often quiet in classes because they have internalized the belief that their experiences are not valid. One student explained her silence in class by saying, "I don't really have much to say. The American kids have had a lot of really interesting experiences. Lots of them have been to Europe and stuff."[17] Significantly, this student uses the term *American* to refer only to White students. Although she was born in the United States, she clearly has internalized the idea that she is not fully American in the same way most of her classmates are.

THE MODEL MINORITY STEREOTYPE

According to the model minority stereotype, Asian Americans have achieved academic, social, and economic success through hard work and adherence to Asian cultural norms. Unlike many stereotypes, the model minority designation seems at first to be positive and even flattering. A close examination of this stereotype, however, reveals its damaging effects both for Asian Americans and for other people of color. First, the stereotype denies the fact that some Asian Americans continue to struggle against structural and other barriers. Second, it has been used as a political weapon against other marginalized groups of color.

Many of the early articles that perpetuated the model minority stereotype several decades ago explicitly compared Asian Americans, who were described as hardworking and successful, with other racial minorities, who were often depicted as lazy welfare cheats. An example of such an article appeared in a December 1966 issue of *U.S. News & World Report*. The authors praised Chinese Americans for "moving ahead on their own—with no help from anyone" and chastised those who "proposed that hundreds of billions be spent to uplift Negroes and other minorities."[18] Asian Americans were considered good citizens precisely because the dominant culture saw them as a passive, quiet minority who did not challenge the status quo. By contrast, African Americans and other racial minorities were cast as loud and demanding complainers who were looking for a handout. In short, adherents to the model minority stereotype used examples of Asian American success to support their claim that equal opportunity existed for all races and that groups who fail have only themselves to blame.

Teachers and other education professionals commonly evaluate Asian American students according to the standards of the model minority. While there is evidence that Asian Americans do well academically as a group, this lumping together of numerous Asian ethnic groups hides the variation in academic achievement across groups and among individuals.[19] Students able to live up to the standards are held up as examples for others to follow, and those unable to meet them are deemed failed or substandard Asians. In my research on Hmong American students at a high school in the Midwest, I found that educators identified many Southeast Asian American students as failing to achieve model minority performance.[20] "An East Asian student might be number three in the class, going to Yale, but the Southeast Asians aren't very motivated," one counselor said.[21] Here, the "success" of East Asian American (i.e., model minority) students is used against the Southeast Asian American youth to cast the latter as underachievers.

Like the perpetual foreigner stereotype, the notion of the model minority also affects interracial relationships. At a high school in a large northeastern city, I found educators who used the model minority stereotype against African Americans and other groups of color.[22] In response to evidence that Black students were the most likely population to drop out or experience failure at Academic High School (a pseudonym), teachers and administrators pointed to the success of Asian American students as "proof" that the system was not racist. In comparing the aspirations of the school's Asian American and African American students, one counselor said, "Asians like U. of P. [University of Pennsylvania], M.I.T., Princeton. They tend to go to good schools. . . . I wish our blacks would take advantage of things instead of sticking to sports and entertainment."[23]

The model minority stereotype also influences perceptions about race among Asian American students. Those who believe the stereotype are likely to assume that they are the superior minority. At Academic High I found that Asian American students who internalized this stereotype often held overtly racist attitudes toward their African American peers.[24] Conversely, the stereotype also led African American students to resent their Asian American counterparts. One African American student explained, "A lot of people I know don't like Asian people because they are intimidated by their intelligence. They say, 'They [Asians] came over here and they bought everything and now look at them in school.'"[25] According to this student's description, his peers see Asian Americans as excellent students (i.e., model minorities), but also as greedy people who go into Black neighborhoods and take over businesses. Like many of the Asian American students at Academic High, the majority of African American students believed that the interests of Asian Americans and the interests of African Americans were at odds.

THE IMPACT OF THE MODEL MINORITY STEREOTYPE
ON ASIAN AMERICAN IDENTITY

The model minority stereotype places a lot of pressure on Asian American students to do well in school. At Academic High, I found that both high- and low-achieving students experienced a great deal of anxiety over their ability to achieve to model minority standards.[26] Some low-achieving Asian American students were so ashamed about their academic struggles that they hid their difficulties from teachers and peers. Many high achievers lived in fear that they were not doing well enough. One high-achieving student remarked:

The [Whites] will have stereotypes, like we're smart. . . . They are so wrong; not everyone is smart. They expect you to be this and that, and when you're not . . . [shakes her head]. And sometimes you tend to be what they expect you to be and you just lose your identity . . . just lose being yourself. [You] become part of what . . . what someone else want[s] you to be. And it's really awkward, too! When you get bad grades, people look at you really strangely because you are sort of distorting the way they see an Asian. It makes you feel really awkward if you don't fit the stereotype.[27]

As this student's comments illustrate, the model minority stereotype shapes not only the way others perceive Asian American students but also these youths' perceptions of themselves.

On the other hand, some Asian American students resist the model minority stereotype entirely because they fear that it marks them as being "nerdy" or "uncool." Male students may fear that being cast as a model minority makes them appear unmasculine. Sometimes these young men exhibit stereotypically masculine traits in order to reject the nerd image of the model minority. Unfortunately, these young men often believe that they must resist school in order to appear manly. One young man at Academic High who affected a sort of hypermasculinity in response to the model minority stereotype explained, "I'm not a wimp. I can defend myself. A lot of Asians can't fight, so they have to go around in gangs. They're small—you know Asian guys." Although this student succeeded at not being seen as a nerd, his attitude toward schooling earned him a place at the bottom of his graduating class.

CONCLUSIONS AND RECOMMENDATIONS

Both the perpetual foreigner stereotype and the model minority stereotype impose limitations on Asian American students that negatively affect their schooling experiences. The perpetual foreigner stereotype excludes Asian Americans from their rightful place as Americans and marks them as inferior to White Americans. The model minority stereotype denies problems within Asian American communities, ignores the continuing inequality faced by Asian Americans, and reinforces the myth of equal opportunity.[28]

Although schools currently play an active role in perpetuating these and other stereotypes, they also contain the seeds of potential change. Schools can make curricular changes that can disrupt and challenge these stereotypes. In literature classes, for example, students can read autobiographies and works of fiction by Asian American authors in order to see which stereotypes are confirmed or challenged by the stories. By teaching the long and complex history of Asian Americans in this country, schools can combat the stereotype of Asian Americans as perpetual foreigners. Information about the historical roots of the foreigner and model minority stereotypes and about the political uses of these stereotypes can be incorporated into discussions of American history. Finally, students need a truly multicultural curriculum that challenges the idea that Asianness and Americanness are mutually exclusive categories. These changes, though seemingly small, could represent, for both Asian American students and the larger school community, the first steps toward broader and more encompassing change.

NOTES

1. Mia Tuan, *Forever Foreigners or Honorary Whites? The Asian Ethnic Experience Today* (New Brunswick, NJ: Rutgers University Press, 1998).
2. Stacey J. Lee, *Unraveling the "Model-Minority" Stereotype: Listening to Asian American Youth* (New York: Teachers College Press, 1996); Keith Osajima, "Asian Americans as the Model Minority: An Analysis of the Popular Press Image in the 1960s and 1980s," in Gary Y. Okihiro, Shirley Hune, Arthur A. Hansen, and John M. Liu (eds.), *Reflections on Shattered Windows: Promises and Prospects for Asian American Studies* (Pullman: Washington State University Press, 1988), 165–174; Robert H. Suzuki, "Education and the Socialization of Asian Americans: A Revisionist Analysis of the 'Model Minority' Thesis," *Amerasia Journal* 4 (1977): 23–51.
3. See *Unraveling the "Model-Minority" Stereotype* and other works by Stacey J. Lee: "More Than 'Model Minorities' or 'Delinquents': A Look at Hmong American High School Students," *Harvard Educational Review* 71, no. 3 (Fall 2001): 505–528; "Learning 'America': Hmong American High School Students," *Education and Urban Society* 34, no. 2 (2002): 233–245.
4. Tuan, *Forever Foreigners*.
5. Tuan, *Forever Foreigners*.
6. Tuan, *Forever Foreigners*, 137.
7. Ronald Takaki, *Strangers From a Different Shore: A History of Asian Americans* (New York: Penguin Books, 1989).
8. Lee, *Unraveling*.
9. A. Lin Goodwin and Maritza B. MacDonald, "Educating the Rainbow: Authentic Assessment and Authentic Practice for Diverse Classrooms," in A. Lin Goodwin (ed.), *Assessment for Equity and Inclusion: Embracing All Our Children* (New York: Routledge, 1997), 211–228.
10. A. Lin Goodwin, *Growing Up Asian in America: A Search for Self* (Greenwich, CT: Information Age Publishing, 2003); Lee, *Unraveling*.
11. Lee, *Unraveling* and "More Than 'Model Minorities'"; Laurie Olsen, *Made in America: Immigrant Students in Our Public Schools* (New York: New Press, 1997).
12. Lee, *Unraveling* and "Learning 'America.'"
13. Lee, *Unraveling*.

14. Lee, *Unraveling*, 46.

15. Stacey J. Lee and Sabina Vaught, "You Can Never Be Too Rich or Too Thin: Popular Culture and the Americanization of Asian American Women," *Journal of Negro Education*, forthcoming (2003).

16. Lee, "More Than 'Model Minorities,'" 51.

17. Lee, "Learning 'America,'" 243.

18. "Success Story of One Minority Group in the U.S," *U.S. News & World Report*, December 23, 1966, 73–78.

19. Valerie O. Pang, "Asian American Children: A Diverse Population," in Donald T. Nakanishi and Tina Y. Nishida (eds.), *The Asian American Experience: A Source Book for Teachers and Students* (New York: Routledge, 1995); Wendy Walker-Moffat, *The Other Side of the Asian American Success Story* (San Francisco: Jossey-Bass, 1995).

20. Lee, "Learning 'America'"; Walker-Moffat, *The Other Side*.

21. Lee "Learning 'America,'" 523.

22. Lee, *Unraveling*.

23. Lee, *Unraveling*, 78.

24. Lee, *Unraveling*.

25. Lee, *Unraveling*, 99.

26. Lee, *Unraveling*.

27. Lee, *Unraveling*, 59.

28. Osajima, "Asian Americans."

Profile

"Desde entonces, soy Chicana":
A Mexican Immigrant Student Resists
Subtractive Schooling

ANGELA VALENZUELA

In a three-year study of immigrant and non-immigrant youth attending Seguín High School (a pseudonym), an overcrowded, segregated, inner-city school in Houston, Texas, I observed the existence of powerful pressures for immigrants to rapidly assimilate, or "Americanize." I explore this pattern in my book, *Subtractive Schooling: U.S.-Mexican Youth and the Politics of Caring.*[1] There I argue that the Americanization of immigrant students' identities results from the way the curriculum at Seguín High School is organized—and not organized. Specifically, the educational process fails to promote bilingualism, biculturalism, and biliteracy. Instead, schooling is more about subtracting than adding these competencies, and in so doing compromises the achievement of immigrant and non-immigrant youth alike.

Most of the youth I interviewed for the study were members of the "1.5 generation," those who had immigrated from Mexico at an early age but who, for the major part of their young lives, had a U.S. schooling experience and were thus similar in many respects to their more acculturated, U.S.-born Mexican American peers. I conclude that recent immigrants' rush to claim a new identity renders them marginal not only with respect to the academic mainstream, but also with respect to their families' social identities.

The rapid assimilation of first-generation immigrant youth is often a sign of maladjustment, because identity "choices" are based on a disaffirmation of the self and of the family's social identity. While I observed this pattern, however, I also observed that some students are able both to assimilate *and* to learn to value the cultural assets that they bring to the schooling context. Nelda was one such student from whom we can learn a great deal.

NELDA

I first encountered Nelda, an eleventh grader, through her English teacher, an Anglo female, who insisted that I meet her. The teacher found Nelda to be a phenomenal student because she had arrived in the U.S. only three years earlier (in eighth grade) and was already a high achiever. Nelda was virtually fluent in English and blended in well socially with the other students in the class. The teacher was most impressed with the fact that, except for a "very mild" accent, Nelda seemed little different from "the others" (i.e., U.S.-born youth) in the way she carried herself. Explaining to Nelda my interest as a researcher, the teacher prepared her for my morning visit to her class.

When I arrived, the students were busy working at their desks. Nelda saw me and, after a nod from the teacher, stepped out into the hall with me, where we talked for the greater part of the 50-minute period. Our conversation began with questions about her background. The entire conversation took place in English, with Nelda occasionally asking me to translate certain words for her.

Nelda said that she was from the interior of Mexico but had lived for several years in Matamoros, Tamaulipas, which is adjacent to the city of Brownsville at Texas' southernmost border. She explained that her family was lured to the U.S.-Mexican border by the availability of industrial jobs. The pay was still low, however, and to make ends meet her mother crossed the border daily into Brownsville, where she worked as a cleaning woman in various homes. Nelda's family lived in Matamoros for five years, where Nelda and her younger sister had the opportunity to attend *secundaria* (middle school). An English-language course was offered at the school one year, but the instruction was very poor. Nevertheless, Nelda appreciated the opportunity to plow through the assigned book for the course. The family's continuing economic struggles ultimately drove her father to seek better-paying construction jobs in Houston. Her mother still works cleaning homes.

I next asked Nelda which subjects she liked the most in school. This question sparked an immediate intellectual exchange. Nelda began by saying that she has always been interested in history, but especially Mexican and Mexican American history. She said that she had always wondered if the relationship between Mexico and the United States parallels that between Anglos and Mexicans in Texas. "Well, what do you think?" I asked. "I think it is very similar," she said. She went on to explain very articulately that Mexico is a poor country compared to the United States and that Mexican Americans are poor compared to Anglos, "though they are richer here than they are in Mexico." Already the budding scholar, Nelda said that she wanted to read and study more to find out why this parallel exists. Nelda also said that she would love to attend college and continue with her interest in history.

I then asked Nelda whether her parents were educated, where her interest in history came from, and how she acquired native-like fluency in English in such a short period of time. She told me that her father had attained a *secundaria* level of schooling, while her mother had received no more than a primary education: "They both had to work to support their families. Life is very hard in Mexico."

Regarding her interest in history and her facility with English, Nelda explained that living on the border and having a lot of exposure to Chicanas/os, hearing the English language, and reading books in English influenced both her thinking and her language fluency. Her mother's experiences as a cleaning woman were pivotal. She explained that in Brownsville her mother worked for many years for a middle-class Mexican American woman. The woman frequently gave Nelda's mother books in English as gifts, which were soon passed on to Nelda. Nelda said she welcomed the opportunity, dictionary in hand, to improve her literacy in English. She recalled reading such authors as Isabel Allende and Laura Esquivel in English. Most important, however, was her discovery of Rodolfo Acuña's book, *Occupied America*, which provides a historical perspective on the taking of the southwestern lands formerly owned by the Mexican government.[2] "*Desde entonces, soy Chicana,*" she said. ("Since then, I am Chicana.") Interestingly, this was the only complete sentence she said in Spanish during any of our interviews.*

Given the vexed relationship between immigrants and Mexican Americans, her comment about being Chicana stunned me at the time. The actual terms *Chicana* and *Chicano* were rarely used as self-identifiers by Mexican American students at Seguín, much less by immigrant females. U.S.-born students prefer to refer to themselves as Mexican Americans, Mexicans, or Hispanics. Our hallway discussion was thus more enlightening for me than

---

*In her use of the term *Chicana*, Nelda identifies herself not only with her own biculturalism (which began with her experience living along the U.S.-Mexico border), but also with the Chicano movement ideology of seeking social justice and a right to self-determination for Mexican Americans.

for her, though I did jot down on a piece of paper some additional readings that I thought she could locate in the public library.

Nelda said she often talked with her parents at home about how possible it was for Mexican Americans to become middle class. Although she was exposed to a lot of criticism about Chicanas/os, even in her own family, Nelda felt that through reading history she had come to see their struggles as her own. Nelda further explained that while she will always consider herself Mexican, she sees herself as different from other Mexicans who "look down" on Chicanos. Thus, she manages the dual identities of Mexican and Chicana without seeing any conflict between the two.

THE EXCEPTION OR THE RULE?

Nelda's case strongly suggests the role that ideology can play in mediating the assimilation of adolescents. Armed with excellent literacy skills and empowering historical knowledge, Nelda demonstrated the capacity both to achieve and to blend in within her social milieu. I later wondered why she was not placed in the honors or magnet level of the curriculum. I speculated that, like the vast majority of immigrant students, she had been tracked into regular-level courses during her first year in middle school.

While living on the border and being exposed to Chicanas/os were contributing factors, these are arguably not sufficient for any immigrant to assimilate as rapidly as Nelda seems to have done. Such contexts abound wherever Mexicans and Mexican Americans are concentrated, yet rapid assimilation within a three-year period is nevertheless exceptional. Clearly, Nelda's passion for history and her desire to understand more fully the sources of both Mexicans' and Chicanas/os' oppression was gripping. The fact that she bore at least some of the emblems of Americanized speech, dress, and interpersonal skills is a side note to a more central awakening within her that helps explain her rapid transformation into a Chicana against the historical and institutional odds of her doing so.

While it is impressive that Nelda was able to arrive at an in-depth understanding of the Mexican American experience, it is unfortunate that she represents the exception rather than the rule. Indirectly, her case embodies an implicit critique of the more general pattern of subtractive schooling, wherein a child's opportunity to develop her or his existing knowledge base is virtually nonexistent. Most significantly, Nelda's case reveals how schools can support a positive sense of identity for immigrant students in ways that are "additive" and empowering. When immigrant youth, and indeed all

Mexican American youth, are allowed to maintain their cultural identities—even if that means deliberately exploring the distinct challenges they can expect to face as bicultural people—they can develop an enhanced sense of efficacy and personal control over their futures and reap immense psychic, social, emotional, and academic benefits.

NOTES

1. Angela Valenzuela, *Subtractive Schooling: U.S.-Mexican Youth and the Politics of Caring* (Albany: State University of New York Press, 1999).
2. Rodolfo Acuña, *Occupied America: A History of Chicanos*, 3rd ed. (New York: HarperCollins, 1988).

CHAPTER FOUR

"Who am I as a learner?"

Would Girls and Boys Tend to Answer Differently?

MICHELLE GALLEY

So many theories about why boys and girls achieve academically at different levels have been put forth in recent years that some have dubbed the verbal jousting the "gender war" in education. First schools were shortchanging girls; then it was the boys who were getting left behind. Even as some arguments grew heated, it was clear that educators needed to do more to address gender differences. But what exactly? How do gender differences play out in the emerging identities of adolescents, and how do these differences affect them both as people and as learners?

The answers to these questions are almost too numerous to count and can vary greatly, depending on whom you ask. Carol Gilligan's groundbreaking book, *In a Different Voice: Psychological Theory and Women's Development,* fired what some saw as the first shots in this gender war when it was published in 1982.[1] At a time when many in the feminist movement were insisting that there are no differences between men and women, Gilligan, a longtime faculty member of the Harvard Graduate School of Education and now a professor at New York University, theorized that there are fundamental and important differences between the sexes. In subsequent work Gilligan expanded her exploration of these differences and focused specifically on how they play out for adolescent girls. She found in her research that as girls entered their preteen years they became unsure of themselves, even if they were previously daring, perceptive, and outspoken in the ways they communicated and acted. They became more focused on what they were "supposed to do," even if that differed from what they knew was right. Gilligan theorized that in order to maintain relationships with others—often those they were expected to please, including teachers and boys—adolescent girls would sacrifice "relationship" with themselves.[2]

More shots were fired on the education front when the American Association of University Women (AAUW) issued the influential—and highly controversial—report entitled *How Schools Shortchange Girls: The AAUW Report, A Study of Major Findings on Girls and Education.* The report claimed that schools were geared more toward educating boys than girls. It also said the books schools used were male oriented and had more male role models and central characters; in essence, they were more supportive of boys' identities than girls'. In addition, the report noted that teachers called on boys more often and suggested that girls were taught to view themselves as less capable of working in the highest-paying professions. Girls were discouraged from taking courses that could eventually lead to lucrative jobs, the researchers charged. They believed that the "glass ceiling" women faced in the job market was also found in classrooms across the country.[3]

Not long after that report was released, research showed that girls were scoring lower on math and science standardized tests. Those test scores were used as further evidence that boys were being better served in schools. More recently, however, girls have started to close the gap in scores on these tests. Recent results show that as high school seniors, girls are trailing boys by an average of only four percentage points on the National Assessment of Educational Progress (NAEP) mathematics test.[4] Even more impressively, girls are excelling on the NAEP reading tests, with twelfth-grade females scoring an average of fifteen points higher than their male counterparts. That number went up five percentage points between 1992 and 1998.[5] This finding is not unique to the United States; in many countries around the world, girls score significantly higher than boys on language arts tests.[6]

Partly fueled by such test scores, the gender war has shifted fronts in recent years to include concerns about boys. Perhaps the best-known writer about the difficulties boys face in school and elsewhere in their lives is William Pollack of Harvard University, who cites the disproportionate number of boys in special education as one piece of evidence that schools are not as "boy friendly" as they could be.[7] (Males make up about two-thirds of the special education population in U.S. public schools.) According to Pollack, the curriculum in most schools is set up in a way that is friendlier to girls than boys. Boys have a natural learning tempo that is more action oriented and hands on than girls', Pollack says, but because most curricula require students to work independently and quietly, many boys end up feeling like failures.

While these theories and research findings may seem difficult to reconcile, one fact seems to emerge from all of them: There *are* differences between boys and girls in school. As the research suggests, many of these differences may be related to the ways boys and girls see themselves as learners, what might be called their "learner identities." There are, of course, countless exceptions that remind us of the need to put such generalities in perspective. (Pollack, for example, would never argue that *all* boys' learning styles are ill served by schools.) Still, it is important for educators to consider some of the patterns that researchers have observed in the different learner identities of boys and girls. This will help teachers and administrators envision classroom environments that might yield the greatest success for both.

A BIOLOGICAL BASIS?

By the time young people reach adolescence they have had years of educational experiences influenced both by biological factors and by the ways society socializes boys and girls. According to Michael Gurian, author of the book *Boys and Girls Learn Differently*, many of the differences in the ways boys and girls develop as learners can be traced back to their brain functions.[8] Girls' brains mature earlier than boys', Gurian says, which is why they are, on average, able to read earlier and speak with better grammar. He notes that girls are also able to hear, smell, and feel tactile sensations better; have better overall verbal abilities; and are better able to control their impulses than boys because of differences in the ways their brains are wired. According to Gurian, those differences result in girls being less likely to take risks and cause boys to be more likely to show a tendency toward aggressive behavior, both of which greatly affect how they see themselves and interact with others in the school context. (See "'I am not insane; I am angry,'" by Michael S. Kimmel, pp. 69–78, and "Male Adolescent Identity and the Roots of Aggression: A Conversation with James Garbarino," pp. 79–83, in this volume.)

On the other hand, because the male brain tends to have better development in the right hemisphere, boys have more advanced spatial abilities on average, according to a study released in the fall of 1999 by researchers at the University of Chicago.[9] The Chicago researchers found that differences in girls' and boys' spatial abilities show up by age four and one-half and are manifest in tasks such as interpreting graphs and maps and in understanding geography. In addition, boys tend to rely on nonverbal communication, which Gurian says has enormous ramifications for them in an education system that relies so heavily on conversation and words.

These factors and a host of others are bound to have an effect on how children view themselves as learners: the extent to which they connect to and like school, how they see their place in the social environment with both teachers and peers, and whether they believe they are "good at" certain subjects or tasks. Because teenagers spend so much of their time together at school, Gurian notes that outside the family, school is the primary identity development system for adolescents: "By the time we turn fifteen, we've expanded the palette or canvas of our identity development well outside our parents."[10]

DIFFERENT VIEWS OF SUCCESS AND FAILURE

One difference in boys' and girls' identities as learners is reflected in the way they view success and failure, according to research by Janice Streitmatter, a professor of educational psychology at the University of Arizona. Boys, Streitmatter says, tend to see failure as something that is caused by external factors and is unstable, "that there is some reason other than themselves that caused the failure." For example, to explain why he performed poorly on an exam, a boy might say that his teacher wrote a bad test, that he was unlucky, or that he was just having a bad day. The cause of his failure has relatively little to do with his actions and is more tied to the education system or factors beyond his control. However, when adolescent boys succeed, they have more of a tendency to identify that success as internal and stable. They say things like, "Of course I aced that test. I knew the material." In other words, boys have a relatively easy time taking credit for their victories.

Girls, on the other hand, seem to do the reverse, says Streitmatter. When girls do well on a test—particularly in math and science—they tend to report that maybe the exam was easy or that they just got lucky that day. And if they don't do well they say that they have never been good at that subject, or that it is just very difficult for them. Streitmatter notes, "Even girls who are in upper-level math classes, like Advanced Placement geometry, tend to hold to this pattern."

What kind of learner we become can be influenced by how we view ourselves in relation to our educational achievements and challenges. If we think that we are just random victims of bad tests when we fail, for example, we might be less invested in our learning. Therefore, teachers may need to help some boys understand that failure is often just as much a result of their own doing as success. On the other hand, seeing success as something random could be just as damaging, so it is vital for girls to take ownership of their successes and learn to appreciate when they have performed well.

SEEING SCHOOL AS RELEVANT

Boys' and girls' identities as learners are also revealed in the degree to which they see school as relevant to their everyday lives. Research has found that boys in particular can have a difficult time finding practical uses for school, especially in the subjects of reading and writing. And, as any observant teacher can tell you, a student who sees course content as irrelevant to "real life" is one who is more reluctant to learn.

In the book *Reading Don't Fix No Chevys: Literacy in the Lives of Young Men*, researchers Michael W. Smith and Jeffrey D. Wilhelm describe their study of the reading habits of forty-nine boys from different academic, ethnic, and socioeconomic backgrounds. Smith and Wilhelm found that even though many of the boys they interviewed valued school, they rejected reading because they saw it as something they had to do for no immediately apparent reason. Even when teachers told them that they needed to pass their classes in order to go to college, for example, the boys still failed to see the importance of that because college, to them, was far off in the future. What mattered most to them was what was happening right then and there. When the boys talked about the experiences with reading that they enjoyed, these were connected to their lives in some concrete way. One boy complained to the researchers that his girlfriend read romances. When asked what was wrong with that, the boy replied, "You can't fix a toilet when you're done."[11]

Smith and Wilhelm also found that the boys tended to look for a sense of "flow" in their activities. The state of flow, originally conceived by psychologist Mihaly Csikszentmihalyi, is one "in which people are so involved in an activity that nothing else seems to matter."[12] Csikszentmihalyi used eight principles to define that experience, which Smith and Wilhelm have combined into four: a sense of control and competence, a challenge that requires an appropriate level of skill, clear goals and feedback, and a focus on the immediate experience.

Most of the boys Smith and Wilhelm studied experienced flow outside of school, often when they were playing video games. This was in part because they felt like they had control over the activity and its outcome, the researchers note. In school, however, many of the boys reported that they never felt in control and that this alienated them from their studies. For example, some felt they never really mastered one activity before they were asked to move on to another one. Wilhelm says that "the very structure of school is contradictory to the elements of flow" and that this circumstance has an effect on the way boys see themselves in connection to learning.

MAKING CONNECTIONS DIFFERENTLY

The girl reading the romance novel in the earlier anecdote was obviously not expecting it to have a practical, immediate application. Researchers have noted that girls are generally able to stick to subjects for longer periods of time and are less distracted from them than boys. They also are far less likely than boys to be diagnosed with attention-deficit/hyperactivity disorder (AD/HD). Girls are therefore more willing to be patient with a lesson even if it doesn't pertain to their everyday lives or seem to give them immediate benefits. This focus seems to give girls at least one kind of edge in school.

But there may be other aspects of schooling that run counter to girls' identities as learners, say researchers Frances A. Maher and Janie Victoria Ward, in their book *Gender and Teaching*.[13] They say the teaching styles prevalent in too many schools are based on competition, thus making them less conducive to girls' success. "Pedagogies built on competitive hand waving silence the quieter students, particularly the girls," Maher and Ward write, because often it is boys who do most of the hand waving.[14] Girls are able to garner more information and make more connections from discussion than from trying to find the absolute right answer, they note.

Not only do girls have the problem of trying to make their way through a competitive school environment, but entering puberty also pulls them in a different direction. For example, Gilligan has found that the pressures of trying to succeed academically by speaking up, but also trying to be attractive to boys by staying quiet, can cause girls to silence themselves in school. Citing Gilligan, Maher and Ward note, "Beginning with puberty, girls 'fall silent' as they try to meet the contradictory expectations of pleasing others, accommodating male standards for female attractiveness and docility, and yet succeeding academically."[15]

Interestingly, however, even in some single-sex classrooms girls still remain relatively quiet. Kathryn Herr, an associate professor of education at the University of New Mexico in Albuquerque, spent the 1999–2000 school year studying 1,100 students—boys and girls—who were being educated in single-sex classrooms at a public middle school in Long Beach, California. In many of the girls-only classes, just a few of the girls spoke up and took leadership roles, says Herr. Some teachers thought these classes were successful because there were no disruptions. But "a quiet classroom is not necessarily the ideal, and we can't equate that with an equitable education," Herr says. Perhaps the pressure of still being in the same school, and thus the same social setting, as boys caused the girls to stay silent in class. Or perhaps the teaching methods used in those classes did not encourage group discussion. Whatever the reason, it is obvious that just excluding young men did not in and of itself cause girls to speak out more.

Interestingly, while taking boys out of the classroom may not have done much to bring out the voices of girls, teaching boys separately did seem to have some benefits, Herr found. The boys she studied who were educated in single-sex classes felt that they could take more risks in class and in making friends. They reported that it felt like a release to be in classes without girls and said that they asked questions they might not have felt comfortable asking if girls had been in the room. Thus, boys were better able to express their learner identities, including being able to speak freely and take risks, in classes that did not include girls.

A WORD OF CAUTION

Of course, as every teacher knows, each student is an individual. Although there are many similarities that researchers have observed among students with certain defining characteristics, such as gender, it is dangerous to oversimplify the issue. Not all boys are alike, nor are all girls alike. Wilhelm and Smith claim that the battle lines in the gender war are misdrawn because there are boys and girls on both sides. They write, "Though people often must necessarily think in generalizations and categories, these are always too simple. Many girls excel in math; many boys love to read. We categorize for the sake of argument, clarity, and for ease of thinking, but sometimes our categories cause problems and keep us from seeing the students before us."[16]

While it is important to note that young women are generally less likely than boys to speak up in class and tend to perform better than boys in reading and writing, that does not mean that every adolescent girl fits into that category. Such assumptions would surely fail those girls who need extra help with literacy skills and falsely define the ones who are natural leaders. Likewise, researchers note that boys tend to respond better to hands-on learning opportunities and perform better in science and mathematics. That does not mean, however, that in science and math classes one should assume that every boy will perform well. Finally, the fact that boys in Herr's study felt freer to take risks does not mean that single-sex classes are a panacea or that they enable all boys and girls to express themselves fully as learners in school.

A struggling student needs extra attention, regardless of gender. What this research tells us, however, is that if a student is not achieving to her or his full potential, educators might consider the ways in which issues related to gender may play a part.

NOTES

1. Carol Gilligan, *In a Different Voice: Psychological Theory and Women's Development* (Cambridge, MA: Harvard University Press, 1982).
2. One of several works in which Gilligan reports these findings is a book she co-authored with Lyn Mikel Brown, *Meeting at the Crossroads: Women's Psychology and Girls' Development* (Cambridge, MA: Harvard University Press, 1992).
3. American Association of University Women, *How Schools Shortchange Girls: The AAUW Report. A Study of Major Findings on Girls and Education,* research by the Wellesley College Center for Research on Women (Washington, DC: AAUW Educational Foundation, 1992).
4. National Assessment of Educational Progress (NAEP) 2000 Mathematics Assessments (Washington, DC: National Center for Education Statistics).
5. National Assessment of Educational Progress (NAEP) 1992, 1998 Reading Assessments (Washington, DC: National Center for Education Statistics).
6. Organisation for Economic Co-operation and Development (OECD), *Knowledge and Skills for Life: First Results from PISA 2000* (Paris: OECD, 2001).
7. William Pollack, *Real Boys: Rescuing Our Sons from the Myths of Boyhood* (New York: Henry Holt, 1998).
8. Michael Gurian, *Boys and Girls Learn Differently! A Guide for Teachers and Parents* (San Francisco: Jossey-Bass, 2001).
9. Susan Levine, Janellen Huttenlocher, Amy Taylor, and Adela Langrock, "Early Sex Differences in Spatial Skill," *Journal of Developmental Psychology* 35, no. 4 (November 2002): 940–949.
10. Quotations in this chapter are from interviews with the researchers, except where noted.
11. Michael W. Smith and Jeffrey D. Wilhelm, *Reading Don't Fix No Chevys: Literacy in the Lives of Young Men* (Portsmouth, NH: Heinemann, 2002).
12. Smith and Wilhelm, *Reading,* 28.

13. Frances A. Maher and Janie Victoria Ward, *Gender and Teaching* (Mahwah, NJ: Lawrence Erlbaum Associates, 2002).

14. Maher and Ward, *Gender and Teaching,* 93.

15. Maher and Ward, *Gender and Teaching,* 93.

16. Smith and Wilhelm, *Reading,* 9.

Profile

Writing Their Way Through: Adolescent Girls and Note Writing

THERESA SQUIRES COLLINS

Many researchers in the latter part of the twentieth century lamented what they saw as the neglect of the adolescent female. Girls, they wrote, were silencing themselves, drowning in a girl-hating culture, and generally being forgotten in schools.[1] By contrast, the advent of the twenty-first century has produced a new crop of writers who classify girls in a different way, based on the allegedly aggressive social habits they exhibit in school. Instead of silenced and forgotten wallflowers, they see overly aggressive young women manipulating one another for social status.

These conflicting views of girls give us reason to step back from overly simplistic characterizations of their behavior and experiences. While it may be tempting to lump girls into categories such as "queen bee," "wannabe," or "alpha girl," the lives of girls defy labeling in many ways.[2] One way girls express who they are, beyond the facile labels, is through note writing. As a teacher-researcher studying the note-writing practices of adolescent girls, I have come to appreciate this activity, which most teachers and other adults find frivolous, as one that helps girls navigate the academic and social changes that are vital to their developing sense of self at this important juncture in their lives.[3]

School is the place where the personal meets the academic. Obviously, course work is of paramount importance in an adolescent's school life, but because middle and high schools are also places where girls develop into young women, the impact of the hundreds of social interactions they have during the course of any day cannot be ignored. Many girls make space for their friendships and for other concerns in their busy lives by writing notes to each other in class. Adolescent boys also write notes occasionally, though the purpose of their writing is almost always in response to a note received from a female acquaintance or girlfriend.

Though many of the girls who participated in my study admitted that they feel compelled to write a note to a friend as soon as they have finished reading one, few believed that writing notes interfered with their class work. Instead, many felt that writing a note alleviated the social tension they were experiencing and allowed them to regain focus. In this way, girls negotiate the reality of how social life and academic life are intertwined. As one of my respondents explained, "If your mind's not there [in class], it'll do no good to try and concentrate—write it [the note] and get back to class with the conflict off your mind; at least you know that the person will know your feelings, and then you can do your work." Another concurred, saying simply, "Either way, it's on your mind, so you might as well write about it and get it off."

Note writing, in addition to freeing up cognitive space, can be a key factor in helping girls discover the primacy of relationships as they make sense of who they are and what's important to them. Notes from friends are, as one of my respondents said, a "casual reminder of everyday life . . . little things that most people wouldn't think of but that make you feel good when you read them in a note." For example, in a note to her friend Kate about planning a disruptive "revolution" in French class, Jessica writes a friendly postscript: "Sorry, but I have to break the military talk to inform you that you look cute today." The note is simultaneously mischievous and supportive, subversive and sweet, and, as in most cases, is concerned with the maintenance of the friendship.

Conversely, notes can also be a place where girls work out their feelings about the difficult life transitions that take place as they mature, including ending friendships that have run their course. This kind of conflict is illustrated in the following excerpt from one respondent's note to a longtime friend:

> For me I entirely believe that absence makes the heart grow fonder and I want to be able to say that that was true in our case. Time and timing is everything to me. And I need time because now is not our time. Also, I think you need to figure out why you are after my friendship and many other ones and figure out if the reasons are valid. Also, please figure out what would actually make you truly happy and work to achieve that. . . . Whatever happens I will always love you, I will never forget you, and I hope that I never can say, "I don't know Kat anymore."

Notes also can be an outlet through which girls discover different parts of themselves. They may draw on artistic sensibilities, experiment with emergent voices, play with conventions of style, and defy the oppressions of the classroom. For example, as girls compose letters to one another, they sometimes use writing techniques that are more sophisticated than any they've used in a required paper; their notes contain passages that are vivid and heartbreaking as well as vicious and hilarious. One girl in my study prided herself on her "Technicolor notes," written in several colors of ink and enjoyed for their cleverness by friends throughout the day. Jessica and Kate created an elaborate cartoon/story series in their notes that chronicled the trials and tribulations of a beleaguered high school girl.

In a particularly poetic exchange, eighth graders Fern and Jo-Jo gave each other—without comment or explanation of subject matter—photographs they had taken. Each girl then pasted the photographs into a notebook and wrote a poem in response. The resulting two books of their original poetry, they said, reflect their creativity as well as "where we were mentally that year." Many of the photographs are of singular images that suggest solitude or a desire for calm, such as a bird in flight or the Lake Michigan shoreline at dusk. The girls have kept these books now for four years and look back at them from time to time to remember how far they've come since their middle school years. Having separated as friends in the transition between middle and high school, the two girls have recently reconnected as friends and as budding poets.

Adolescent girls' notes reveal that they are coping together with stresses and issues that, in very significant ways, are central to their middle and high school experiences. This is not to say that notes take care of every emotional and social need that girls have, or that girls do not need caring adults in their lives to assist with difficult times. Still, note writing shows girls' spirit, independence, and solidarity in the face of the difficult transition of adolescence.

Girls obviously do not think about their identity development in the same way that adult theorists do, but their notes reveal that they are thinking about more than gossip. The act of note writing is prevalent within classrooms—almost so common that it becomes invisible. We need to take seriously the things that girls do independently in school to help them navigate through the minefield of cliques, tests, passing periods, and social traumas.

"They are our food," remarked a girl I interviewed. Notes give their readers "a chance to know that someone was thinking about you that day," as one student put it, and they can assure a girl that she will make it through a particularly rabid bout with the rumor mill. They praise good grades, a goal scored, and a date made, and in so doing they help girls foster one another's positive self-esteem. Notes are the arbiters of disagreements between friends and enemies alike. They are colorful and creative, coded in case they fall into enemy hands. More often than not, these messages written on 8½ x 11-inch notebook paper are binding missives that chronicle an adolescent girl's most meaningful thoughts, feelings, and relationships within the context of the school day.

NOTES

1. Mary Pipher, *Reviving Ophelia* (New York: Putnam, 1994); Myra Sadker and David Sadker, *Failing at Fairness: How America's Schools Cheat Girls* (New York: Charles Scribner's Sons, 1994); Peggy Orenstein, *Schoolgirls: Young Women, Self-Esteem, and the Confidence Gap* (New York: Doubleday, 1994); American Association of University Women/Wellesley College Center for Research on Women, *How Schools Shortchange Girls: A Study of Major Findings on Girls and Education* (Washington, DC: AAUW Educational Foundation, 1992).
2. Rachel Simmons, *Odd Girl Out: The Hidden Culture of Aggression in Girls* (New York: Harcourt, 2002); Rosalind Wiseman, *Queen Bees and Wannabes: Helping Your Daughter Survive Cliques, Gossip, Boyfriends, and Other Realities of Adolescence* (New York: Crown, 2002).
3. For my 1995 master's thesis at Northwestern University ("Handwritten with Care: A Study of Girls' Notewriting in School"), I conducted an ethnographic study of this practice among high school girls at Evanston Township (Illinois) High School. Though the sample of girls whose interviews were used in the paper numbered three, I conducted group interviews throughout the year and collected, read, and categorized more than two thousand notes. All quotes from interviews and notes come from my thesis. With the exception of Jessica and Kate, who granted permission to use their names, all other names were omitted or changed.

CHAPTER FIVE

"I am not insane; I am angry"[1]

Adolescent Masculinity, Homophobia, and Violence

MICHAEL S. KIMMEL

Violence in our nation's schools has emerged as one of our most gripping social problems. All over the country, Americans are asking why some young people open fire, killing or wounding other students and their teachers. Are these teenagers emotionally disturbed? Are they held in the thrall of media-generated violence—by video games, the Internet, rock or rap music? Are their parents to blame? Our shock and concern, and the wrenching anguish of parents who fear that their children may not be safe in their own schools, demand serious policy discussions. And such discussions demand serious inquiry into the causes of school violence.

In November 2000, the FBI released its report of all twenty-eight cases of school shootings in the United States since 1982.[2] These cases—in which a young student opens fire, apparently randomly, and shoots teachers and students—are the only type of school violence that has increased since 1980.[3] This followed two earlier government studies: the Surgeon General's *Report on Youth Violence* and the Bureau of Justice Statistics' *Indicators of School Crime and Safety 2000*. These were followed quickly by a major new study of bullying behaviors.[4] Clearly, questions about safety and school violence are of pressing national concern.

All these studies, however, concentrated on identifying potential anteced-
ents of school violence; for example, media influence, drug and alcohol use,
Internet usage, and family dynamics and structure. They paid little or no attention to the fact that *all* the school shootings were committed by boys.
This uniformity cut across all other differences among the shooters: some
came from intact families, others from single-parent homes; some boys had
acted violently in the past, others were quiet and nonsuspect; some boys expressed rage at their parents (two killed their parents the same morning),
and others seemed to live in happy families.

For a contrast, imagine what these studies would have examined had it
been girls who had committed all the shootings: Would not gender be the
only story? The single greatest risk factor in school violence is masculinity.
The analytic blindness of previous work runs even deeper than gender. All
but one of the thirty-eight school shootings were committed by White boys
who lived in the suburbs. As a result, the public has assumed that these boys
were deviants, their aberrant behavior explainable by some psychopatholo-
gical factor.

While this is no doubt true, at least in part—the boys who committed
these terrible acts probably did have serious psychological problems—such
a framing also masks the way race and class play a significant role in school
violence. Again, imagine if all the school shooters had been poor African
American boys in inner-city schools. It is unlikely that our search for causes
would have pathologized the boys as much as the culture of poverty or the
"normality" of violence among inner-city youth.

Still, most students—White or non-White, male or female—are not violent, schools are predominantly safe, and school shootings are aberrations.
As a public, we seem concerned with school shootings because the story is
not one of simply "when children kill" but, specifically, when suburban
White boys kill.

ASKING THE RIGHT QUESTIONS

There were four cases of school shootings documented between 1982 and
1990; there were twenty-four cases in the 1990s. Figure 1 presents a map of
the United States with the sites of these shootings marked. It is immediately
apparent from this map that school shootings don't occur uniformly or
evenly in the United States, which makes one skeptical of uniform cultural
explanations such as violent video games, musical tastes, the Internet, or
television and movies. School shootings are *not* a national trend. Of the

Figure I Sites of Documented School Shootings in the United States, 1982–2001

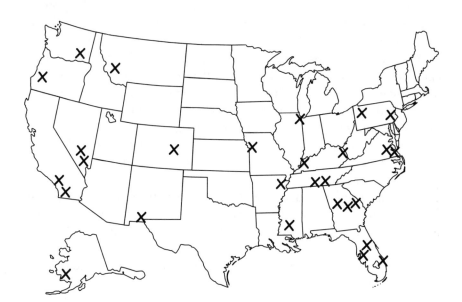

twenty-eight school shootings between 1982 and 2001, all but one (in Chicago) were in rural or suburban schools. All but two (in Chicago and Virginia Beach) were committed by White boys. In addition, twenty of the twenty-eight school shootings took place in states that voted for George W. Bush in the 2000 presidential election. Among the other shootings, one was in suburban Oregon, one was in rural eastern Washington State, two were in Southern California, one was in rural and another in suburban Pennsylvania, and one was in rural New Mexico.

Of course, all of this does not suggest that rural and suburban Whites who vote Republican are responsible for school violence. But it does suggest that school violence is unevenly distributed, and that understanding it requires that we look locally at the factors that accompany political affiliation, particularly in rural and suburban areas. We need to look at local "gun culture" (percentage of homes owning firearms, gun registrations, NRA memberships), and at local gender culture and school cultures—attitudes about gender nonconformity, tolerance of bullying, and teacher attitudes. We need to focus less on the form of school violence—documenting its prevalence and presenting a demographic profile of the shooters—and more on the *content* of the shootings, asking questions instead about family dynamics and composition, psychological problems and pathologies, local school cultures and hierarchies, peer interactions, prevailing gender ideologies, and the interactions among academics, adolescence, and gender identity.

What we have ignored is a striking consistency in the stories that have emerged about the boys who did commit the violence. All had stories of being constantly bullied, beat up, and, most significantly for this analysis, "gay-baited." All seem to have been mercilessly and constantly teased, picked on, and threatened. And, most strikingly, it was *not* because they were gay (none of them was gay as far as we can tell), but because they were *different* from the other boys—shy, bookish, an honor student, a "geek" or a "nerd." Theirs are stories of cultural marginalization based on criteria for adequate gender performance, specifically the enactment of codes of masculinity. (By contrast, boys in inner-city schools are structurally marginalized by racism and income inequality; their violence often takes a different form.)

This chapter reports some preliminary findings from my investigation of these issues. I locate the causes of school violence in the constellation of adolescent masculinity, homophobia, and other gender-related factors that may help us understand—and prevent—school violence before it occurs.[5]

TAKING AWAY THEIR MANHOOD

Before beginning any inquiry, it's often helpful to ask an expert. When confronted recently about his homophobic lyrics, the rap star Eminem offered the following explanation. Calling someone a "faggot" was not a slur on his sexuality, but on his gender: "The lowest degrading thing that you can say to a man when you're battling him is to call him a faggot and try to take away his manhood. Call him a sissy. Call him a punk. 'Faggot' to me doesn't necessarily mean gay people. 'Faggot' to me just means taking away your manhood."[6]

In this rationalization, Eminem perhaps unwittingly addresses the central connection between gender and sexuality, and particularly the association of gender nonconformity with homosexuality. Homophobia is far less about the irrational fear of gay people or the fear that one might actually be gay or have gay tendencies, and more the fears that *heterosexuals* have that others might perceive them as gay.[7] The terror that others will see one as gay, as a failed man—the fear I call homophobia—underlies a significant amount of men's violence. Put another way, homophobia might be called "the hate that makes men straight."

There is much at stake for boys during adolescence, and heterosexual boys engage in a variety of evasive strategies to ensure that no one gets "the wrong idea" about them. These strategies range from the seemingly comic (though telling)—such as two young boys occupying three movie seats by placing their coats on the seat between them—to the truly tragic, such as engaging in homophobic violence, bullying, excessive risk taking (drunk or aggressive driving), and even sexual predation and assault. The impact of homophobia is felt not only by gay and lesbian students, but also by heterosexuals who are targeted by their peers for constant harassment, bullying, and gay-baiting. In many cases, gay-baiting is "misdirected" at heterosexual youth who may be somewhat gender nonconforming.

As we examined all available media reports of these school shootings, a striking picture emerged. In the overwhelming majority of these cases there were also reports that the boys were teased and bullied mercilessly by classmates, that they were constantly called "faggot," "homo," and "queer." For example, young Andy Williams, who shot several classmates in Santee, California, was described as "shy" and was "constantly picked on" by others in school. (They stole his clothes, his money, and his food, beat him up regularly, and locked him in his locker, among other daily taunts and humiliations.)[8] Classmates described Gary Scott Pennington, who killed his teacher and a custodian in Grayson, Kentucky, in 1993, as a "nerd" and a "loner" who was constantly teased for being smart and wearing glasses.[9] Barry Loukaitas, who killed his algebra teacher and two other students in Moses Lake, Washington, in 1996, was an honor student who especially loved math; he was also constantly teased and bullied and described as a "shy nerd."[10] And Evan Ramsay, who killed one student and the high school principal in Bethel, Alaska, in 1997, was also an honor student who was teased for wearing glasses and having acne.[11]

Fourteen-year-old Michael Carneal was a shy and frail freshman at Heath High School in Paducah, Kentucky, barely five feet tall, weighing 110 pounds. He wore thick glasses and played in the high school band. He felt alienated, pushed around, and picked on. He was said to be very upset when students called him a "faggot" and almost cried when the school gossip sheet labeled him as "gay." On Thanksgiving 1997, he stole two shotguns, two semiautomatic rifles, a pistol, and 700 rounds of ammunition, and, after a weekend of showing them off to his classmates, brought them to school hoping that they would bring him some instant recognition. "I just wanted the guys to think I was cool," he said. When the "cool" guys ignored him, he opened fire on a morning prayer circle, killing three classmates and wounding five others. Now serving a life sentence in prison, Carneal told psychiatrists weighing his sanity, "People respect me now."[12]

At Columbine High School, the site of the nation's most infamous school shooting, this connection was not lost on Evan Todd, a 255-pound defensive lineman on the Columbine football team, an exemplar of the "jock" culture that Dylan Klebold and Eric Harris found to be such an interminable torment. "Columbine is a clean, good place, except for those rejects," Todd said. "Sure we teased them. But what do you expect with kids who come to school with weird hairdos and horns on their hats? It's not just jocks; the whole school's disgusted with them. They're a bunch of homos. . . . If you want to get rid of someone, usually you tease 'em. So the whole school would call them homos."[13] In the videotape made the night before the shootings, Harris said, "People constantly make fun of my face, my hair, my shirts." Klebold added, "I'm going to kill you all. You've been giving us shit for years."

What Klebold said he had been receiving for years apparently included constant gay-baiting, being called "queer," "faggot," "homo," being pushed into lockers, grabbed in hallways, mimicked and ridiculed with homophobic slurs. For some boys, high school is an interminable torment, a constant homophobic gauntlet, and they may respond by becoming withdrawn and sullen, using drugs or alcohol, becoming depressed or suicidal, or acting out in a blaze of overcompensating, violent "glory."[14] The prevalence of this homophobic bullying, teasing, and violence is staggering. (See "Growing Up in the Shadows" by Michael Sadowski, pp. 85–101, in this volume.)

My hypothesis is decidedly *not* that gay and lesbian youth are more likely to open fire on their fellow students. In fact, from all available evidence, *none* of the school shooters was gay. But homophobia—being constantly threatened and bullied *as if they were* gay, as well as the homophobic desire to make sure that others knew that they were not gay—seems to play a significant and understudied role in these school shootings.

Still, several key questions remain. I've already suggested that the first question to ask is, why boys? But more specifically, why White boys? Today we explore "masculinities" to denote differences among boys and men based on race, class, region, age, and sexuality. Failure to see race while looking at gender often makes us miss the real story. We know that African American boys face a multitude of challenges in schools—from racial stereotypes to formal and informal tracking systems, low expectations, and underachievement. But the one thing they do not do is plan and execute random and arbitrary mass shootings. And this is particularly interesting, since the dynamics of the classroom and academic achievement have different valences for African American girls and African American boys. In their fascinating ethnographies of two inner-city public high schools, both Signithia Fordham and Ann Ferguson discuss these differences. When African American girls do well in school, their friends accuse them of "acting White," but when African American boys do well in school, their friends accuse them of "acting like girls."[15]

Perhaps cultural marginalization works itself out differently for subordinates and superordinates, the privileged and the unprivileged. Even if they are silenced or lose their voice, subordinates—women, gays and lesbians, students of color—can tap into a collective narrative repertoire of resistance, "the ongoing narrative of the struggle for racial equality."

White boys who are bullied are supposed to be real men, supposed to be able to embody independence, invulnerability, manly stoicism. The cultural marginalization of the boys who committed school shootings extended to feelings that they had no other recourse. They felt they had no other friends to validate their fragile and threatened identities; they felt that school authorities and parents would be unresponsive to their plight; and they had no access to other methods of self-affirmation.

WHY THESE PARTICULAR BOYS?

There have to be some reasons why school shootings take place in these places and not others, as well as why these boys, and not others, become perpetrators. Obviously some boys—many boys—are routinely picked on, bullied, and gay-baited in schools across the country on a daily basis. How do they cope? What strategies do they use to maintain their composure, their self-esteem, and their sense of themselves as men?

David, a student who had been victimized by bullies at school, was interviewed recently for a *Time* magazine story about resilient youth. For David, the bullying started when he was thirteen: "At first I tried to brush it off. But it got worse. I got beat up every day and couldn't take it. I'd fake being sick. My grades slipped." His parents tried to intervene with school officials, but the attacks continued. David's thoughts got darker:

I felt, "What did I do to deserve this?" I wanted revenge. I never sat down and planned anything—-I personally couldn't pick up a gun and kill someone, it's not who I am—but I will tell you I did want to hurt them. I wanted them to feel how bad I felt.[16]

But he didn't. Most boys who are bullied, harassed, and baited survive—as do their classmates. Several possible factors may help explain this. Perhaps there is a "charismatic adult" who makes a substantial difference in the life of the child. Most often this is a parent, but it can also be a teacher.

Perhaps the boy can develop an alternative pole around which he can experience and validate his identity. Bullying suggests that the boy is a failure at the one thing he knows he wants to be and is expected to be—a man. If there is something else that he does well—a private passion, music, art, someplace where he feels valued—he can develop a pocket of resistance.

Similarly, the structures of a boy's interactions can make a decisive difference. A male friend, particularly one who is not also a target but seems to be successful at masculinity, can validate the boy's sense of himself as a man. As one male high school student commented, "If you go to school and people make fun of you every day, and you don't have a friend, it drives you to insanity."

But equally important may be the role of a female friend, a potential if not actual "girlfriend." Five of the school shooters had what they felt was serious girl trouble, especially rejection. It may be that the boys who are best able to resist the torments of incessant gay-baiting and bullying are those who have some girls among their friends, and perhaps even a girlfriend—that is, girls who can also validate their sense of masculinity (which other boys do as well) *as well as* their heterosexuality (which boys alone cannot do).

The successful demonstration of *heterosexual* masculinity—which is the foundation, after all, of gay-baiting—requires not only successful performance for other men, but also some form of "sexual" success with women. (I put the word "sexual" in quotation marks because this doesn't necessarily mean actual sexual contact but rather a sexualized affirmation of one's masculinity by girls and women. If the girl is not a "girlfriend" she is at least a girl and a friend, and therefore a potential romantic and sexual partner; therefore the boy can assume some degree of heterosexual competence.)

These sorts of questions—the dynamics of local culture, the responsiveness of adults and institutions, and the dynamics of same-sex and cross-sex friendships—will enable us to understand both what led some boys to commit these terrible acts and what factors enable other boys to develop the resources of resistance to daily homophobic bullying.

Take a walk down any hallway in any middle school or high school in America. The single most common put-down today is, "That's so gay." It is deployed constantly, casually, unconsciously. Boys hear it if they dare to try out for school band or orchestra; if they are shy or small, or physically weak and unathletic; if they are smart, wear glasses, or work hard in school. They hear it if they are seen to like girls too much, or if they are too much "like" girls. They hear it if their body language, their clothing, or their musical preferences don't conform to the norms of their peers. And they often hear it not as an assessment of their present or future sexual orientation but as a commentary on their masculinity.

Eminem had at least this part right: Calling someone a "faggot" means questioning his manhood. And in this culture, when someone questions our manhood, we don't just get mad, we get even.

NOTES

1. Luke Woodham, age sixteen, perpetrator of school shooting in Pearl, Mississippi.
2. Mary Ellen O'Toole, *The School Shooter: A Threat Assessment Perspective* (Quantico, VA: National Center for the Analysis of Violent Crime, FBI Academy, 2000).
3. See Barry Glassner, "School Violence: The Fears, the Facts," *New York Times*, August 13, 1999, as well as Glassner's book, *The Culture of Fear* (New York: Basic Books, 1999).
4. Tonja R. Nansel, Mary Overpeck, Ramani Pilla, June Ruan, Bruce Simmons-Morton, and Peter Scheidt, "Bullying Behaviors among U.S. Youth: Prevalence and Association with Psychosocial Adjustment," *Journal of the American Medical Association* 285, no. 16 (2001): 2094–2100.
5. This ongoing research is being undertaken with Matt Mahler in the Department of Sociology at the State University of New York at Stony Brook.
6. Cited in Richard Kim, "Eminem—Bad Rap?" *The Nation*, March 5, 2001.
7. Michael S. Kimmel, "Masculinity as Homophobia: Fear, Shame and Silence in the Construction of Gender Identity," in Harry Brod and Michael Kaufman (eds.), *Theorizing Masculinities* (Newbury Park, CA: Sage, 1994).
8. Kristen Green and Bruce Lieberman, "Santana Gunman Targeted with Anti-Gay Epithets," *San Diego Union-Tribune*, March 10, 2001.
9. Jerry Buckley, "The Tragedy in Room 108," *U.S. News & World Report*, November 8, 1993.
10. "Did Taunts Lead to Killing?" *Minneapolis Star Tribune*, February 4, 1996.
11. Steve Fainaru, "Alaska Teen's Path to Murder," *Dallas Morning News*, December 4, 1998.
12. Jonah Blank, "The Kid No One Noticed," *U.S. News & World Report*, October 12, 1998.

13. Nancy Gibbs and Timothy Roche, "The Columbine Tapes," *Time*, December 20, 1999, 50–51.

14. Timothy Egan, "Patterns Emerging in Attacks at Schools," *New York Times*, June 15, 1998.

15. Signithia Fordham, *Blacked Out: Dilemmas of Race, Identity, and Success at Capital High* (Chicago: University of Chicago Press, 1996); Ann Ferguson, *Bad Boys: Public Schools in the Making of Black Masculinity* (Ann Arbor: University of Michigan Press, 2000).

16. Robert Sullivan, "What Makes a Child Resilient?" *Time*, March 19, 2001, 35.

Interview

Male Adolescent Identity and the Roots of Aggression: A Conversation with James Garbarino

DARCIA HARRIS BOWMAN

James Garbarino has done extensive research into the issues that affect boys and men in contemporary society, including why a disturbing number of boys behave in ways that are aggressive and sometimes even violent. Garbarino is a professor of human development and director of the Family Life Development Center at Cornell University. He also has authored or coauthored seventeen books, including Lost Boys: Why Our Sons Turn Violent and How We Can Save Them *and, with Ellen deLara,* And Words Can Hurt Forever: How to Protect Adolescents from Bullying, Harassment, and Emotional Violence.

What has your work with violent boys taught you about the link between male adolescent identity and aggressive behavior?

I've learned that there's a culturewide problem, that the definition of male identity is wrapped up in three messages: that it's better to be mad than sad, that to be a man is to be powerful and strong, and that aggression is a legitimate way of responding to conflict and problems. Vulnerable and otherwise at-risk boys are likely to combine these three cultural themes with their own difficulties—family troubles, psychological problems, poverty—and are therefore at a high risk for aggressive or violent behavior.

What about boys who don't necessarily fall into this "at-risk" category?

These cultural principles apply to all boys, but most don't ever bring them all together in the form of extreme violence. Boys who don't have obvious social risk factors like poverty, exposure to racism, or family disruption may nonetheless be at high risk because they carry with them psychological troubles that predispose them to negative behavior. When that's coupled with the three cultural themes, they may act in aggressive or violent ways.

And, certainly, the average level of violence and aggression is higher for boys than it is for girls. Much of that is related to these cultural issues of identity. There are institutional forms of aggression that are particularly tied to male identity. An example would be in ice hockey, where they make rules for boys and men that give permission, even encouragement, for a high level of aggression, whereas rules for women in ice hockey preclude precisely that particular kind of behavior.

Are boys genetically hardwired for aggression and violence, or is such behavior solely an expression of how boys are socialized?

I think boys on average are predisposed genetically to patterns of behavior and arousal that make them more vulnerable to learning aggression if it's taught. The fact that boys are more physically aggressive than girls in virtually every culture in the world suggests that boys are more ready than girls to learn and demonstrate aggressive behavior.

But the fact that American girls are more aggressive than boys in some other societies would suggest that, while the average within a society may very well be a function of gender, the average across societies is mainly a matter of culture and experience. But will girls ever get to a point in America where they are as aggressive as boys? I, and I think most people, would be startled if that happened.

In your book *Lost Boys: Why Our Sons Turn Violent and How We Can Save Them*, you use the term *progressive conformity* to describe how human behavior is a reflection of what is learned, encouraged, and rewarded in a given social context. What do boys learn about violence and aggression in the school setting, and how do these messages influence their behavior?

A school, like any setting, is a social context, and that means it can either enhance or inhibit aggressive behavior. We've learned very clearly, for example, that to deal with the issue of bullies is not simply a matter of finding the bullies and stopping them, but also of recognizing that some social systems in schools tolerate and encourage bullying and others encourage less aggressive behavior. The same kid may be four times more likely to be an aggressive bully in one school than in another, and that speaks to the role of context and the validity of the principle of progressive conformity. Kids over time will to a large degree resemble what the setting rewards, models, and accepts. When it promotes positive character traits, most of the kids will fall into line with that. But when it tolerates aggression, that's particularly what the high-risk kids will do. I think the message is that being a male in a school doesn't make you a bully. Being a troubled male makes you more ready to take on the role of bully, but what the school offers has a lot to do with whether you will take on that role or not.

Who *is* the school bully? How does he view himself in relation to his peers, particularly the targets of his aggression, and what prompts his behavior?

There are several pathways to becoming a bully. One is this institutionalized form of bullying. You're a freshman, the seniors haze and bully you, and it becomes the cultural expectation that when you get to be a senior you'll do the same thing. Some boys will relish that role more than others. And all the usual factors that predispose kids to aggressive behavior generally—abuse or deprivation at home, for example—certainly predispose them to come to school and act aggressively. There's also a sort of generational passing on of bullying. Maybe half the kids involved in bullying at any one time have themselves been victims. So there is a violence-breeds-violence side to it as well.

And again, whether or not these predispositions and risk factors translate into bullying seems to depend on the school itself, and that may begin in elementary school. Take research by Shepard Kellum [of Johns Hopkins University] that looked at aggressive kids, particularly boys, who come into first grade and find a weak teacher who allows a chaotic classroom and the formation of aggressive peer groups. By sixth grade, those kids may be twenty times more aggressive than they would have been if they'd walked into first grade and found a strong teacher who took charge of the classroom and didn't allow chaos and the formation of aggressive peer groups.

There's always that social-system dimension to it, and that's really the thing people are least likely to get. They're more likely to see it as a problem of "aggressive individuals are bullies and vulnerable individuals are their victims." Certainly there are influences in that direction, but whether or not it actually happens depends much more on the social system, including the bystanders and what their norms are, what they support, and what they tolerate.

Are there social systems in schools that are particularly culpable when it comes to modeling or teaching aggression to boys, or perhaps some that are helpful in stemming the problem?

I think one important social system within the school is adult monitoring and control. When adults are in evidence throughout the school, that has a suppressing effect on aggression. Secondly, when the school models and rewards competition rather than cooperation, you're more likely to set loose the process of aggression. You see this in the classroom: the activities that are offered, the way academic rewards are structured. Also important is the way the adults in the school deal with issues of the various "isms"—sexism, racism, homophobia. If they give messages that these are acceptable ways to think about people, it is more likely to unleash phobias based on those things, or problems like sexual harassment.

What about the role of school athletics and other extracurricular activities?

I think extracurricular activities play several roles. The more widespread the participation, the more likely you'll get participation across cliques and groups. When diverse groups are involved in cooperative activities—winning a game, painting, performing a concert—that creates cooperative behavior and suppresses aggression.

Now, some of these activities have bullying built into them in the form of hazing. Certainly, there are many stories about how athletics have this problem. That may drive some kids out of these activities and the message becomes, once again, that the adults support bullying.

If the goal is to stem aggressive and violent behavior in boys and socialize them to be caring, considerate, and sensitive, what do schools and educators need to do?

Character education is fundamental to violence prevention, because the theme is "everybody in our school lives by some core values." It's not just "find the bullies and stop them." It's "we all live by the core values, and that makes bullying incompatible with the culture of our school." In addition to the usual meetings and discussion, this is translated into the adults being really on top of things and not tolerating certain behavior in the halls—and their actually being in the halls. A big issue is often that teachers stay in their classrooms during the changing of classes, so the halls become a no-man's land and the kids are on their own out there.

Character education also implies that adults will be responsive when kids or parents report incidents, that they won't simply say, "Look, there's nothing we can do, our hands are tied." So, it's partly an attitude, it's partly specific behaviors, and it's partly implementing programs so that when something happens, you don't just go to the bully and the victim, you go to everyone else who was there and say, "Why did you allow this to happen? Why didn't you make a statement here?"

Is there anything else specific teachers can do?

I think they can be very aware of the fact that the models they present through themselves, as well as in videos, films, and biographies, should show male strength as something other than aggression. Highlighting those qualities is a way of changing the culture in a school.

CHAPTER SIX

Growing Up in the Shadows

School and the Identity Development of Sexual Minority Youth

MICHAEL SADOWSKI

Beginning in middle school, I became really depressed. At first I didn't know why. Didn't have a clue. But I knew it wasn't okay to be gay. No one was out at my middle school, but I heard lots of slurs all the time. Lots of homophobic comments. I was scared. Scared to be a lesbian. Scared to be out at school. Scared of being so alone.

—*Alix M., in* Hatred in the Hallways[1]

For a long time I always felt pretty good about myself. I was captain of our high school soccer team, pretty high up in my class, and really popular with just about everybody. At the end of my junior year, I won the "best looking" and "most likely to succeed" awards. But then I started drinking. At first I thought I was just being cool—you know, one of the guys—but then I knew that I was drinking because I *didn't* feel like one of the guys. It took me a long time to realize it, but for three years I'd had a crush on this other kid on the soccer team. . . . I thought that if I told my friends about falling in love with another guy, they'd start calling me "faggot" and stop hanging out with me. I thought that maybe I wasn't gay anyway. So instead of telling my friends or doing anything else about it, I just started to drink a real lot.

—*Jackson, in* Real Boys[2]

Psychologists have long considered adolescence a time of tremendous personal growth and transition. Erik Erikson, the adolescent psychology pioneer whose work is probably the most widely cited in the field, believed that young people experience the "crisis" of identity formation most acutely during adolescence.[3] They strive to know and accept who they are, which involves trying to establish a positive sense of self and envisioning a future role for themselves in adult society. A virtually universal aspect of this self-definition process is adolescents' keen awareness of how others perceive them. Indeed, any parent or teacher could likely echo Erikson's finding that adolescents are "morbidly, often curiously preoccupied with what they appear to be in the eyes of others as compared with what they feel they are."[4]

As the stories of Alix and Jackson illustrate, for youth who are sexual minorities,* the gulf between how they wish to be perceived "in the eyes of others" and "what they feel they are" can be enormous and difficult to navigate. While individual experiences vary, researchers have found that many lesbian, gay, and bisexual youth become aware of homosexual feelings roughly between the ages of ten and twelve[5] and begin to understand these feelings as homosexual or bisexual, at least on some level, by around age fifteen.[6] (Far less is known about when students might begin to identify themselves as transgender.) Some sexual minority adolescents, often those in the most supportive environments, "come out" as lesbian, gay, bisexual, transgender, and/or queer during high school or even middle school.[7] Others, however, respond to the expectation that their true identities will not be accepted by acting "straight": dating heterosexually, changing their physical appearance or behavior to suit society's gender expectations, possibly even rejecting others whom they perceive to be gay.[8] For both "out" youth and their closeted peers, coming through the crisis of adolescent identity success-

---

*When discussing the issues that affect youth who are lesbian, gay, bisexual, or transgender (LGBT), language is a problematic issue. Until recent years, most studies referred only to gay and lesbian youth, but researchers have become increasingly aware that bisexual people are a distinct group with specific concerns. More recent research also has recognized the special issues affecting transgender youth and adults, those who do not conform to traditional man/woman or boy/girl gender norms in a variety of ways. (Some transgender youth also identify as gay, lesbian, or bisexual, while others do not.) In addition, some adolescents identify as "queer," a designation that implies a rejection of societal norms around sexuality and gender, or "questioning," if they are unsure of their sexual orientation or gender identity. When speaking of the studies in general, I use the terms *lesbian, gay, bisexual,* and/or *transgender,* the abbreviation *LGBT,* or the term *sexual minority youth.* When citing specific studies, I use the terms the researchers used to describe the specific populations they sampled.

fully—establishing a self-accepting and optimistic answer to the question, "Who am I?"—is often fraught with special challenges.

Alix's and Jackson's statements also show how powerful school environments and peer culture can be in the self-definition process of sexual minority youth, as well as the risks these adolescents face coming of age in a world that is not ready to accept them. For Alix, the struggle of coming to terms with being a lesbian is accompanied by depression and fear of the school environment. Jackson resorts to heavy drinking as he tries to reconcile his homosexual feelings with the very real possibility of rejection from his peers.

Unfortunately, Alix's and Jackson's experiences are far from unique. A growing body of research shows that sexual minority youth are at disproportionate risk for depression and substance abuse, as well as a number of other negative outcomes both in and out of the school environment. The most recent Massachusetts Youth Risk Behavior Survey (MYRBS), which includes the responses of more than four thousand youth from randomly selected high schools around the state,[9] found that sexual minority youth (those who identified themselves as lesbian, gay, or bisexual, or said they had had same-sex sexual contact) were significantly more likely than their peers to have felt "sad or hopeless" for two weeks or more (49% vs. 28%).[10] They also were more likely to have used various illegal drugs, to have engaged in behaviors that can lead to alcohol abuse, and to have skipped school because they felt unsafe.

The most consistent—and most disturbing—finding about these youth is the disproportionate number who report suicidal ideation and behaviors. The 2001 MYRBS found that, among the roughly 5 percent of students identified as lesbian, gay, or bisexual, nearly one out of three (31%) had attempted suicide in the past year. This figure is nearly four times higher than the 8 percent reported for other students.[11] The MYRBS also found far greater incidence among sexual minority youth of seriously considering suicide, making a suicide plan, and requiring medical attention because of a suicide attempt, and these data are supported by previous versions of the study as well as other research that shows much higher rates of suicidality for this group.[12]

While it is obviously difficult for researchers to establish causal links between the experiences adolescents have in the school environment and risk factors such as suicidality and substance abuse, there is at least evidence to suggest that school climates contribute in some powerful ways—many of them negative—to lesbian, gay, bisexual, and transgender adolescents' sense of who they are.

ANTI-LGBT LANGUAGE AND HARASSMENT

Spend five minutes in any middle or high school in the United States and you're likely to hear at least one of the many verbal slurs commonly used against sexual minorities: "Fag!" "Homo!" "Queer!" "Dyke!" A recent survey by the Gay, Lesbian and Straight Education Network (GLSEN), taken among 904 lesbian, gay, bisexual, and transgender (LGBT) youth in forty-eight states and the District of Columbia, found that 84 percent of these youth heard such homophobic remarks either "frequently" or "often" in their schools. Even more common, the respondents said, was the expression "That's so gay," a pejorative term used widely by adolescents to describe virtually anything perceived to be negative—a boring class, an ugly article of clothing, an unfair grade on a test. Ninety-one percent of the youth GLSEN surveyed said they heard that expression (or the variant, "You're so gay") at school "frequently" or "often."[13] Earlier GLSEN studies, as well as research conducted by a number of other organizations, have resulted in similar findings.

Surveys like GLSEN's show how widespread this kind of homophobic language is in schools, and the testimonials of high school students illustrate in more vivid terms how it permeates school cultures. *Hatred in the Hallways*, a 2001 report about U.S. schools by the international advocacy group Human Rights Watch, includes comments by three students who explain just how pervasive antigay language was in their schools:

> "People called everyone 'faggot,'" said Chance M., an eighteen-year-old senior in Massachusetts. "That's like the word of the century. It turned into a routine." "That's how you pick on someone, straight or gay. You call them a fag," said James L., a sophomore in the Los Angeles area. "I hear it a lot of times during the course of the day, a lot, at the very least ten to twenty times a day." "These guys, they'll stand in front of the lockers. They'll be like, 'Look at that faggot.' You hear it every day," Tommy L. told us.[14]

At the very least, this kind of language contributes to an uncomfortable, if not hostile, environment for LGBT students, or those who might be questioning their sexuality or gender identity. Many LGBT students, however, also experience such language in the form of verbal harassment targeted directly at them. More than 83 percent of the youth GLSEN surveyed for its 2001 report said they had been the victims of such verbal harassment in school. Similarly, in a 1999 report entitled *They Don't Even Know Me!* Beth

Reis, director of the Safe Schools Coalition of Washington State, summa-
rizes reports made by targeted youth, their parents, or witnesses to in-school
harassment based on actual or perceived sexual orientation and/or gender
identity. Reis recounts three of these incidents as follows:

> The insults fly from the back of the school bus: "Dyke," "Queer," "Fag-
> got." The offenders are two guys and a girl. They've been harassing two
> particular middle school girls every day for two months now. Today, one
> tells the girls, "We don't want you here."[15]

> Ever since the start of the school year, a seventh grader has been the target
> of daily bullying in the hallways. Among other taunts, the kids call him
> "flute boy" because he plays with the symphony. One student walks right
> up to him and asks, "How come you are so gay? Are you gay?" He says,
> "No," and keeps on walking as if it doesn't bother him. But it does.[16]

> "Get away, Gay Boy!" "Don't let Gay Boy touch you!" For three or four
> months, this second grader hears these taunts from his peers. He's not sure
> why they say this about him or what he's done "wrong." Nobody will play
> with him at recess. He is becoming less excited about school and often pre-
> fers to stay home. While in the classroom, he is more reserved, less interac-
> tive, and less confident and is afraid of some of the bigger kids.[17]

These stories demonstrate how the harassment of students based on sexual orientation or gender identity affects more than just students who are
"out" in their schools. As Reis notes, many of those who are called "fag,"
"dyke," or other such names in school may not even grow up to be lesbian,
gay, bisexual, or transgender. Her data also point to another sobering fact:
that harassment based on perceived sexual orientation and/or gender identity begins very early for some students, in some cases in the early elementary grades. Thus, by the time they reach adolescence, some youth have en-
dured years of taunting and harassment based on the way they are labeled as
first or second graders.

Physical violence against sexual minority youth appears to be somewhat
less pervasive than verbal harassment, but GLSEN's 2001 study still found
that 42 percent of respondents had experienced physical harassment at
school (being pushed or shoved because of their sexual orientation) and that
21 percent had been physically assaulted (punched, kicked, or injured with a
weapon). Moreover, nearly two-thirds (65%) of the students said they'd
been harassed sexually at school, for example, being targets of sexual com-

ments, inappropriately touched, etc. This number was even higher for lesbian and bisexual girls (74%) and for students who identified as transgender (also 74%).

Just what effect this kind of harassment has on youth who are at various stages in their awareness of their sexual and gender identities is difficult to measure. Based on their interviews with 140 youth in seven states, Michael Bochenek and A. Widney Brown, authors of the Human Rights Watch report, conclude that both direct harassment and the general toleration of anti-LGBT language in school environments cause extreme emotional distress for sexual minority students:

> The unrelenting verbal attacks on lesbian, gay, bisexual, and transgender students create a hostile climate that can be unbearable for them. . . . Although the youth we interviewed frequently focused on fear of physical and sexual violence, many noted that the experience of being called "faggot," "queer," dyke," and other slurs on a daily basis was devastating. One gay youth who dropped out of an honors program angrily protested, "Just because I am gay doesn't mean I am stupid," as he told of hearing "that's so gay" meaning "that's so stupid," not just from other students but from teachers in his school.[18]

The MYRBS also has pointed to possible connections between the kinds of stressors sexual minority youth experience at school and increased risk for depression and suicide. The study found that youth who were victimized at school were significantly more likely to report higher levels of depression, more suicidal thinking, and more actual suicide attempts than other students. Moreover, the study also linked suicide ideation and attempts to emotional isolation, an experience reported by many of the sexual minority students interviewed in qualitative studies.

LACK OF REPRESENTATION IN CURRICULUM AND SCHOOL ACTIVITIES

> It's not even in the curriculum. It's like we're not even supposed to know about it. "That's so gay" is the only thing we ever hear about it.
> —*Lauren M., in* Hatred in the Hallways[19]

If the language and harassment LGBT students face make them feel painfully conspicuous at school, the curriculum they are studying may do just the opposite. Despite the fact that many students are aware of homosexuality—or at least the slurs that are associated with it—from the early elementary grades, numerous studies have pointed to a lack of representation of anything having to do with LGBT people in school curricula.

In 1993, Rita Kissen of the University of Southern Maine surveyed forty-four youth, most of whom indicated that homosexuality was never mentioned in any of their classes in high school.[20] Moreover, as Kissen explains:

> Of the 19 "yes" answers, only a few were positive. Several said homosexuality was mentioned in health class, without any context and often in a negative way. One lesbian recalled that her health instructor told the class that homosexuality was a form of mental illness. A student who attended a parochial school said homosexuality was discussed as a sin in his religion class.[21]

Similarly, only three out of twenty-seven respondents to a 1997 survey by Kathleen P. Malinsky recalled any discussion of homosexuality in their schools that was not associated with AIDS.[22] One of Malinsky's participants remembered, "We did condoms, sex, teen pregnancy, suicide, eating disorders, every kind of cancer—you name it, we did it. But nothing on homosexuality."[23] Similarly, the majority of Malinsky's participants said there was no printed information available about homosexuality in the library or anywhere else in the school. While it may be that such information was available and the participants were simply unaware of it, other researchers have noted that information about homosexuality is often kept out of school libraries by officials who wish to avoid controversy.[24]

While Kissen's and Malinsky's studies both rely on small samples and data collected during the 1990s, more recent, larger studies suggest that little has changed. The GLSEN survey found that 81 percent of the 904 students surveyed said there were "no positive portrayals of LGBT people, history, or events in any of their classes." Yet the small percentage of students whose schools did present such positive portrayals were "more likely to feel they belonged in the school" than their peers whose schools did not.

"Students rarely hear anything about issues relating to sexual orientation or gender identity elsewhere [besides health or sex education classes] in the curriculum," note Bochenek and Brown. "If they do hear about someone who is lesbian, gay, bisexual, or transgender, it is almost invariably in a negative light."[25] As the authors go on to point out, many teachers avoid discussing LGBT issues or people in their classes, even when to do so might seem natural and appropriate, for fear of repercussions from administrators and the community. As one teacher they interviewed in West Texas put it,

"My principal would faint [if I discussed LGBT issues in class]."[26] As a result of this kind of self-censoring, many sexual minority youth go to school receiving no information about homosexuality, nontraditional gender identity, or LGBT people other than the slurs they hear under uncontrolled circumstances.

Related to the lack of LGBT representation in curriculum is the often unspoken but very palpable taboo on LGBT issues in other aspects of the school environment. Central to the cultures of most middle and high schools, for example, are proms, dances, and other social events that, more often than not, present opposite-sex attraction and dating as the only possible "normal" option for youth. Similarly, the visible signs of pairing that go on in many school hallways, marked by the hand-holding and other public displays of affection that are seen as a rite of passage in adolescence, are usually exclusively heterosexual. In such a context, students who have same-sex attractions and may even wish to date members of the same sex may find themselves feeling left out (at best) and self-hating and shameful (at worst). In rare but inspiring examples of progress, some same-sex couples are now attending proms or asserting their right to be "out" in the school environment, but most students still find the price of such openness too high. Similarly, the heavily gendered culture of many high schools—where the most respected boys are sports heroes and the most popular girls are cheerleaders—provides little affirmation of the nontraditional gender identity.

LACK OF ADULT SUPPORT AND ROLE MODELS

One of the most consistent findings in psychological research with youth is the importance of caring, trusting relationships with adults. Such a relationship with even one adult has been demonstrated to give children and youth the resilience to cope with some of the difficult experiences they might face growing up.[27] And, as decades of adolescent development research has demonstrated, adolescents need adult role models to help them envision their futures, a central aspect of the identity development process.

Many adolescents find the caring relationships they need with parents or other adult family members. But for sexual minority youth, coming out often means being rejected by their families. In a 1993 study, only 11 percent of youth who disclosed to their parents that they had same-sex attractions reported a positive response, and there is little reason to believe the statistic would be much higher for a study conducted today. The 2001 MYRBS found that sexual minority youth were significantly less likely than their peers to believe they could talk to adults in their family about "things that are important" to them. "Generally, sexual minority youth experience a lack of parental, sibling, and extended family support, which can exacerbate many of the problems they experience," note Deborah Tharinger and Greg Wells of the University of Texas at Austin, who have researched the relational experiences of LGBT adolescents.[28] Tharinger and Wells also point out that when sexual minority youth seek support from their families, the results are sometimes extreme. They cite one 1995 study that found that 10 percent of sexual minority youth were physically assaulted by family members for reasons related to their sexual orientation, and note that lesbian girls may be at the greatest risk in this regard.[29]

Given the unpredictability of parental support for LGBT youth, teachers, counselors, principals, and others in the school environment can play especially important roles. Indeed, many teachers are making crucial, possibly life-saving differences in the lives of sexual minority students who otherwise might be completely lacking in adult support. Unfortunately, however, a number of studies suggest that the attitudes and actions of some educators may be a significant detriment to LGBT youths' ability to develop a positive sense of self. The GLSEN survey found that 40 percent of the youth polled did not believe there were any teachers or counselors in their schools who were supportive of LGBT students. Also, in a 1998 survey of 101 guidance counselors, Janet Fontaine (an expert on counseling issues and LGBT youth) found that most counselors rated teachers' attitudes about lesbian and gay people as less favorable than "neutral."[30]

Several of the students Human Rights Watch interviewed, including Dahlia P., a lesbian student from Texas, and Gerald A., a transgender youth from California, describe in painful detail the negative role unsupportive adults play in their school lives:

> [One of my teachers would] say, "Well, if you weren't a lesbian you might pass this class," or "If you'd get your head out from between those girls' thighs, maybe you'd pass." The message was I would be so much better off if I weren't gay.[31]

> In my social science classes, sometimes topics dealing with sexual orientation or gender identity would pop up, and I'd get put on the spot. . . . Another time, we were talking in class about what each of us would do if we had $70,000, and when it came to me the teacher said, "Oh, I know what you're gonna get." This was for a final project. Mine was really about the Russian economy, but he assumed I was going to write about getting a sex-change operation.[32]

Human Rights Watch also found that administrators, when faced with complaints of harassment by LGBT students, sometimes "blame the victim" and suggest that students who do not conform to expected gender norms are bringing the harassment upon themselves. They cite the example of one gay student who was told by his school's principal, "You chose this lifestyle; you need to carry all the baggage that comes with it,"[33] and an assistant principal who reportedly said of a student who was being harassed, "If he didn't walk around telling people that he's gay, there wouldn't be any problems."[34]

One of the most damaging ways some school staff contribute to the creation of identity-detrimental environments for LGBT youth is in their failure to respond to hostile language and harassment. Eighty-two percent of GLSEN's 2001 survey respondents indicated that faculty and staff "never intervened" or "intervened only some of the time" when they heard anti-LGBT language. Even more disturbing, nearly one-fourth (24%) of the youth surveyed said they had heard faculty and staff *use* such language.

Even school staff who are LGBT themselves may fail to address homophobic language and harassment when they are aware of it for fear of drawing too much attention to themselves and thereby risking their jobs.[35] In thirty-seven states, it is still legal to fire an employee, including a teacher, based solely on her or his sexual orientation, and in forty-nine states transgender people have no laws protecting them if they are fired based on their gender identity.[36] Fortunately, in a growing number of schools, especially those in states and municipalities that outlaw such employment discrimination, more teachers are coming out as lesbian, gay, bisexual, or transgender, providing role models for students who may or may not be prepared to acknowledge their own sexual orientation or gender identity during adolescence.

SPECIAL CHALLENGES FACING LGBT YOUTH OF COLOR

New research is beginning to explore the ways in which sexual minority status and race intersect in the school lives of adolescents. GLSEN's 2001 survey, for example, found that 48 percent of LGBT students of color reported having been verbally harassed because of both their race or ethnicity *and* their sexual orientation. As noted previously, LGBT youth often have few safe places to turn for help in dealing with this kind of abuse. Yet some LGBT youth of color may be especially isolated in this regard, even where school-based support is readily available.

In his analysis of the issues facing queer youth of color at a California high school (CHS), Lance McCready of the University of California at Berkeley notes how the racial and gender composition of groups intended to support LGBT youth may actually be alienating to sexual minority youth of color, leaving these students without the identity affirmation such organizations are intended to provide.[37] McCready, who had been a faculty member at the high school he studied, recalls his first encounter with Project 10, the school's support organization for LGBT students:

> On the day of the Project 10 meeting, I walked into Fran's classroom expecting to see a collage of students that reflected the racial and ethnic diversity that CHS is famous for. Instead of diversity, I found homogeneity: the group was composed of twelve White, female, lesbian and bisexual-identified students.[38]

McCready notes that Jamal, a gay African American student he interviewed, found that Project 10 "was not particularly safe or confidential." Moreover, McCready found peer groupings and activities at CHS to be segregated by race, virtually forcing students like Jamal to choose which aspects of their identities to foreground in their social interactions:[39]

> Jamal recognized that at CHS, where social groups are often defined by race, identifying himself as gay (a social identity he and other Black students perceived as White) in every situation would put him at odds with his Black peers. Consequently, he chose to de-emphasize his sexuality and involve himself in extracurricular clubs and activities (such as student government) that are legitimated by Black students. Downplaying his sexuality also meant that Project 10 was off-limits. Particularly among Black students, to align oneself with Project 10 meant risking harassment and public ridicule.[40]

As Jamal's story illustrates, LGBT students of color can often face rejection from one identity community if they choose to align with another. Again, it is difficult to measure the effects that this "choice among identities" has on these young people. Though research in this area is just beginning to emerge, it suggests—at the very least—that the specific issues facing these adolescents warrant special consideration by educators.

ELEMENTS OF AN IDENTITY-SUPPORTIVE SCHOOL

While there is strong evidence that U.S. schools are not doing enough to help sexual minority students develop a positive sense of identity, there are numerous steps educators can take to effect change in their schools. These steps include, but are certainly not limited to, the following.

Frank discussion of anti-LGBT language and harassment. Perhaps the easiest and most obvious thing educators can do is take active steps toward interrupting and discouraging anti-LGBT language and harassment. While much of the success of such efforts depends on the vigilance and consistency of individual teachers, principals and school leaders also can play an important role in setting a tone of mutual respect and addressing the issue head-on with both staff and students.

Beth Reis, who has facilitated LGBT awareness programs in schools, recommends that at the beginning of each school year principals hold assemblies or class visits in which they frankly discuss the kinds of harassment and bullying that are "not OK" at school. In such presentations, she says, it is critical for school leaders to use terms such as *gay* and *lesbian*, as well as the slurs associated with them, in order to communicate strongly and clearly with both would-be harassers and potential targets: "I think the leadership of having a principal be the one who [talks about anti-LGBT harassment] is critical for every kind of child who's experiencing difference or being bullied," Reis says. "Even if they don't go to an adult when it happens, it means something to know that they could, and to know that the principal knows that this happens sometimes."

Visibility and inclusion. Another benefit to discussing anti-LGBT harassment in specific and frank terms is that such discussion raises the visibility of sexual minority issues at school. On the other hand, only presenting LGBT issues as problems can be damaging to youths' efforts to develop a healthy sense of self. As a starting point toward a more positive approach, educators can use inclusive language when discussing relationships, families, and other issues rather than assume that all students—and their parents, brothers, sisters, or friends—are heterosexual and traditionally gender identified.

Still, as every educator knows, the curriculum is at the center of any student's instructional experience. If a school's curriculum silences lesbian, gay, bisexual, and transgender people and issues, then the isolation with which LGBT students experience this aspect of their identities is exacerbated. In making his case for a gay-inclusive curriculum, Arthur Lipkin, author and former teacher, writes:

> In addition to these pragmatic considerations [including that virtually all students will know and work alongside gay and lesbian people at some

point in their lives], educators should be spurred by their professional duty to impart accurate and complete information in their classes and counseling sessions. Expurgation is dishonesty.[41]

Specific guidelines for an identity-positive (and age-appropriate) curriculum in the various school subjects are beyond the scope of this chapter, but as Lipkin points out, opportunities exist not just in health and sex education, but also in English/language arts, history and social studies, science, the arts, and a variety of other subject areas.

Adult support and role models. As indicated previously, researchers have found that some sexual minority youth receive crucial support from teachers, counselors, and other adults at school. GLSEN's survey found that students who said their schools had a supportive faculty and staff were more likely to feel they "belonged" in school than those who did not. Also, the Massachusetts Department of Education found that sexual minority students who believed there was an adult they could talk to were less likely to skip school, use drugs, or make a suicide attempt than other lesbian, gay, or bisexual youth.[42]

Along with "straight" teachers who show that they are supportive of LGBT youth, LGBT adolescents benefit greatly from "out" teachers and other role models who can represent for them what it means to be a successful LGBT adult. Since Erikson and others have noted that a key part of identity development is the ability to envision a future role for oneself in adult society, such role modeling can be especially meaningful for sexual minority youth, for whom positive portrayals are all but invisible.[43]

"I've heard young adults talk about how there was an openly gay teacher in their school, and they never let the teacher know at the time that they were also gay or lesbian or bi or trans," says Reis. "Yet having that teacher present was the thing that kept them from committing suicide."

Gay-straight alliances. Perhaps the most ubiquitous form of in-school support for sexual minority youth, gay-straight alliances (GSAs) now number more than one thousand in schools across the United States.[44] These groups are cocurricular organizations in which students can seek the support of peers and faculty advisors, discuss issues such as homophobia and heterosexism that might exist in the school and community, and plan programming about sexual orientation and gender identity issues. Fifteen years ago, these organizations were virtually nonexistent, so the research on their effectiveness is extremely new. Still, a few recent studies have resulted in some promising findings.

In an evaluation of the Safe Schools Program for Gay and Lesbian Students, an initiative to support GSAs and other programming administered by the Massachusetts Department of Education, Laura Szalacha found statistically significant differences on several measures between schools that had GSAs and those that did not. Based on questionnaires completed by 1,646 randomly selected students, Szalacha discovered that 35 percent of students in schools with GSAs said gay, lesbian, and bisexual students could be open about their sexual identity in school, compared to 12 percent of students in schools without GSAs. In addition, while 58 percent of students in schools with GSAs said they heard anti-gay slurs every day in school, 75 percent of the students in schools without GSAs said they heard such words daily.[45]

As Reis explains, "GSAs offer kids a safe place to socialize without having to watch your back, without having to worry that something you say will be used against you, without having to pretend to be someone you're not—whether that's social time, just playing Scrabble, or more therapeutic time, having people that you can talk with about having been harassed or about having broken up with your girlfriend or boyfriend."

As McCready's and other studies are beginning to show, however, GSAs can only fulfill their mission of providing a safe, identity-affirming place for all youth if all feel welcome. It is therefore important for any school with a new or existing GSA to consider whether students of all races, ethnicities, genders, social groups, and abilities feel welcome and supported.

THE CHALLENGE AND THE RESPONSIBILITY

It would be naive for any educator to expect that efforts to make a school environment more identity supportive for LGBT students would not meet with some form of community opposition on religious and/or political grounds. Changes in curriculum to include LGBT people and issues, even if made in age-sensitive ways, have prompted especially strong protests in the past.[46] Yet the high rates of suicide, substance abuse, alienation from school, and other negative outcomes that affect LGBT students make the needs of this population difficult to ignore. If noble slogans such as "No Child Left Behind" truly express the charge of American education, then meaningful efforts to support the identities of sexual minority students must be a part of that mission.[47]

NOTES

1. Michael Bochenek and A. Widney Brown, *Hatred in the Hallways: Violence and Discrimination against Lesbian, Gay, Bisexual, and Transgender Students in U.S. Schools* (New York: Human Rights Watch, 2001), 108.
2. William Pollack, *Real Boys: Rescuing Our Sons from the Myths of Boyhood* (New York: Henry Holt, 1998), 207.
3. Erik H. Erikson, *Identity: Youth and Crisis* (New York: W. W. Norton, 1968). Many later researchers have criticized Erikson's model as overly formulaic and lacking regard for such important factors as gender and ethnicity. Nevertheless, Erikson's findings about the identity crisis of adolescence have remained central to the field.
4. Erikson, *Identity*, 128.
5. Anthony R. D'Augelli and Lawrence J. Dark, "Lesbian, Gay, and Bisexual Youths," in Leonard D. Eron, Jacquelyn Gentry, and Peggy Schlegel (eds.), *Reason to Hope: A Psychosocial Perspective on Violence and Youth* (Washington, DC: American Psychological Association, 1995), 177–196.
6. Deborah Tharinger and Greg Wells, "An Attachment Perspective on the Developmental Challenges of Gay and Lesbian Adolescents: The Need for Continuity of Caregiving from Family and Schools," *School Psychology Review* 29, no. 2 (2000): 158–172.
7. For more on queer identity in adolescence, see "Why Use *That* Word?" by Arthur Lipkin, pp. 102–106, in this volume.
8. Tharinger and Wells, "An Attachment Perspective."
9. Youth Risk Behavior Surveys (YRBS) are funded federally by the Centers for Disease Control and Prevention. In addition to the national survey, there are thirty-two state surveys and sixteen surveys administered in various municipalities. Massachusetts is the only state for which the YRBS includes questions specifically about sexual orientation and breaks out data along these lines. (Vermont's study includes some questions about sexual activity, but does not specifically include questions about students' self-identified sexual orientation.)
10. Massachusetts Department of Education, *2001 Massachusetts Youth Risk Behavior Survey [MYRBS] Results 59*, available online (at press time) at www.doe.mass.edu/hsss/yrbs/01/results.pdf
11. Massachusetts Department of Education, *2001 MYRBS Results*.
12. In addition to the Massachusetts Youth Risk Behavior Surveys, a key resource on this topic is Gary Remafedi (ed.), *Death by Denial: Studies of Suicide in Gay and Lesbian Teenagers* (Boston: Alyson, 1994), which includes the results of numerous studies on sexual minority youth suicide.
13. Gay, Lesbian and Straight Education Network (GLSEN), *2001 National School Climate Survey,* available online (at press time) at www.glsen.org/templates/news/record.html?section=20&record=1029
14. Bochenek and Brown, *Hatred in the Hallways*, 33.
15. Beth Reis, *They Don't Even Know Me! Understanding Anti-Gay Harassment and Violence in Schools* (Seattle: Safe Schools Coalition of Washington, 1999), 32.
16. Reis, *They Don't Even Know Me*, 32.

17. Reis, *They Don't Even Know Me*, 30.
18. Bochenek and Brown, *Hatred in the Hallways*, 35.
19. Bochenek and Brown, *Hatred in the Hallways*, 120.
20. Rita M. Kissen, "Listening to Gay and Lesbian Teachers," *Teaching Education 5*, no. 2 (1993): 57–67.
21. Kissen, "Listening," 59.
22. Kathleen P. Malinsky, "Learning to Be Invisible: Female Sexual Minority Students in America's Public High Schools," *Journal of Gay and Lesbian Social Services* 7, no. 4 (1997): 35–50.
23. Malinsky, "Learning," 40.
24. Bochenek and Brown, *Hatred in the Hallways*.
25. Bochenek and Brown, *Hatred in the Hallways*, 120.
26. Bochenek and Brown, *Hatred in the Hallways*, 121.
27. Among the articles frequently cited on this issue is one by Michael Rutter, "Psychosocial Resilience and Protective Mechanisms," *American Journal of Orthopsychiatry* 57, no. 3 (1987): 316–331.
28. Tharinger and Wells, "An Attachment Perspective," 167.
29. Neil W. Pilkington and Anthony R. D'Augelli, "Victimization of Lesbian, Gay, and Bisexual Youth in Community Settings," *Journal of Community Psychology* 23 (1995): 34–56.
30. Janet H. Fontaine, "Evidencing a Need: School Counselors' Experiences with Gay and Lesbian Students," *Professional School Counseling* 1, no. 3 (1998): 8–14.
31. Bochenek and Brown, *Hatred in the Hallways*, 65.
32. Bochenek and Brown, *Hatred in the Hallways*, 62.
33. Bochenek and Brown, *Hatred in the Hallways*, 83.
34. Bochenek and Brown, *Hatred in the Hallways*, 83.
35. Bochenek and Brown, *Hatred in the Hallways*.
36. As this book goes to press, the only states in which it is illegal to discriminate in employment on the basis of sexual orientation are California, Connecticut, Hawaii, Maryland, Massachusetts, Minnesota, Nevada, New Hampshire, New Jersey, New York, Rhode Island, Vermont, and Wisconsin. Minnesota and the District of Columbia have laws protecting against discrimination in employment on the basis of sexual orientation *and* gender identity.
37. Lance McCready, "When Fitting In Isn't an Option, or, Why Black Queer Males at a California High School Stay Away from Project 10," in Kevin K. Kumashiro (ed.), *Troubling Intersections of Race and Sexuality: Queer Students of Color and Anti-Oppressive Education* (Lanham, MD: Rowman & Littlefield, 2001).
38. McCready, "When Fitting In Isn't an Option," 37.
39. See also "'Joaquín's Dilemma'" by Pedro A. Noguera, pp. 19–30, in this volume.
40. McCready, "When Fitting In Isn't an Option," 42.
41. Arthur Lipkin, *Understanding Homosexuality, Changing Schools: A Text for Teachers, Counselors, and Administrators* (Boulder, CO: Westview Press, 1999), 332.
42. MYRBS, unpublished data, 1999.
43. See also Mihaly Csikszentmihalyi and Reed Larson, *Being Adolescent: Conflict and Growth in the Teenage Years* (New York: Basic Books, 1984).
44. *Source*: Gay, Lesbian and Straight Education Network data.

45. Laura A. Szalacha, "The Sexual Diversity Climate of Massachusetts' Secondary Schools and the Success of the Safe Schools Program for Gay and Lesbian Students," doctoral dissertation, Harvard Graduate School of Education (2001).

46. For a discussion of the controversy over the Children of the Rainbow multicultural curriculum proposed for the New York Public Schools, as well as other struggles involving the introduction of LGBT themes in curriculum, see James W. Button, Barbara A. Rienzo, and Kenneth D. Wald, *Private Lives, Public Conflicts: Battles over Gay Rights in American Communities* (Washington, DC: Congressional Quarterly Press, 1997), 146–152.

47. This chapter is based in part on an analysis conducted for my qualifying paper at the Harvard Graduate School of Education, "The Quality of School Life for Lesbian, Gay, Bisexual, and Transgender Adolescents in U.S. Middle and High Schools: A Review of the Research Literature" (2002). Committee members were Jocelyn Chadwick, Michael Nakkula, and Terrence Tivnan, with additional assistance from James T. Sears.

Commentary

Why Use *That* Word? Adolescents and Queer Identity

ARTHUR LIPKIN

> When someone recently whistled in class, the teacher told the student to stop, and then said that only "queers and shipmates" whistle.
> —*From the* Houston Chronicle[1]

> Me and Daniel, we even made a necklace that says "queer" and we used to wear it at school. Everybody would just laugh about it or look at it like, you know, "Wow, they're really open with it." That put them in assurance that you don't have to be scared of us because we're not scared of you.
> —*From the* Orange County Register[2]

A small but growing number of youth whom others might classify as lesbian, gay, bisexual, or transgender (LGBT) are calling themselves "queer." In a recent California survey of high school gay-straight alliances (groups for the support of sexual minority students and the advancement of gay rights), queer-identifying youth made up about 12.5 percent of those who did not identify as "straight." Another 12.5 percent chose "bisexual" to describe themselves; those identifying as "gay" and "lesbian" were evenly divided at 37 percent each.[3]

It is important for educators who might be baffled or discomfited by this "queer emergence" to understand both its political and psychological roots. At its simplest level, adolescents' use of the term *queer* is a public appropriation of a demeaning epithet. Other stigmatized groups have tried to defuse the power of name-calling by transforming hurtful words into prideful ones. The adoption of *nigger* by some African Americans is a good analogue, as is the lesbian embrace of the slur *dyke*.

The word queer originally gained popularity in college and university communities. Besides helping them thumb their noses at insulting homophobes, academics' use of the term *queer* furthered the goal of rejecting what they saw as arbitrary, rigid, and oppressive sexuality labels. They started using the term to undermine the diametric opposites of straight and gay. As a result of this new view of human sexuality, beginning in the 1980s many Gay Studies programs on college campuses came instead to be called Queer Studies. The 1990s activist organization Queer Nation took the name into the streets, and now adolescents have picked up on it as a form of self- and community identification.

Besides representing an attempt to de-fang their tormentors, "queer" offers some youth a relatively comfortable and open-ended way to say that they are "not straight." It is psychologically suitable because, rather than boxing them into a category, it allows possibilities for change and growth. Even as more youth come out at earlier ages as lesbian, gay, bisexual, or transgender, others wait indefinitely in what psychologist Esther Rothblum calls the "lingering" category.[4] Although some hesitate out of internalized homophobia or fear of family and peer rejection and harassment, others wait because they doubt the validity of the lesbian, gay, bisexual, and transgender categories. For them, the emergence of queer is a manifesto of their freedom from this kind of strict sexuality labeling.

For some adolescents, the word queer is more appealing than bisexual, either because they aren't sure of the scope of their attractions or because they reject the latter term's connotations. They are aware that bisexual means "omnivorously promiscuous" to many heterosexuals and "confused or cowering" to many gays. Those judgments, of course, are undeserved. Being open to exploring one's full sexuality is not the equivalent of being oversexed, confused, or frightened.

Queer also encompasses both sexuality and gender, incorporating a spectrum of gender expression that gay, lesbian, and bisexual do not necessarily imply. It recognizes the fundamental trangenderedness of all people who violate conventional male and female norms—in the bedroom, the wardrobe, the schoolhouse, the playing field, and so on. It rejects the oppositional designations of man/woman or boy/girl as the only possibilities.

Moreover, the spaciousness of queer invites community formation among sexual minority youth that was rare a generation ago. As one recent San Francisco high school graduate observed:

> Queer unifies the community. We're so used to being sectioned off into our groups and subcultures. This is one word that embodies all of us. It's some-

thing we are struggling for in the younger generation. It's saying we're all in this together, this is who we are, our history, culture and everything we've been through.[5]

The term can even include adolescents who do not view themselves as sexual minorities but identify as "politically queer," sympathetic to their sexual minority peers, and resistant to dominant cultural values pertaining to sexuality and gender.

Finally, the breadth of queer creates space in the "not straight" community for those who bring a non-Western, non-White perspective to their same gender desires and sexualities. They may resist the terms *gay, lesbian,* or *bisexual* being applied to feelings and pursuits that are understood differently in their native and community cultures. Adopting these labels could estrange them not only from their established sense of themselves but also from their cultural supports, families, and friends who consider such homosexual identities alien. (Of course, multiple-minority people may find queer no less problematic than gay, even if the former is intended to be more accommodating. Native Americans, for example, might favor the term *two-spirit,* or African Americans, *being on the down low.*)

The appropriation of queer does not mean that the word has lost its poison entirely. As with nigger or dyke, context is everything; it's all in who says it and how. From kindergarten on, even the word gay can be a dagger, and schoolyard bullies and other gay bashers haven't discarded the term queer as a weapon. So it is no surprise that a majority of sexual minority youth aren't comfortable with the term queer—at least not enough to apply it to themselves.

The factors that influence anyone's sense of self and determine how one presents oneself to the world are an interdependent matrix. Gender, race, and ethnicity affect one's sexual identity; conversely, sexuality has an impact on one's gendered, racial, and ethnic "selves." As there are many ways to experience and express one's same-gender attractions and experiences, there are a number of corresponding sexual identities. All of them can be subsumed under the word queer and welcomed to the fellowship of sexuality difference. In the end, of course, young people need and deserve to be able to call themselves whatever they want. We should accept their choices with understanding, good humor, and optimism.

NOTES

1. Paige Hewitt, "Seeking Tolerance," *Houston Chronicle,* April 4, 2002.
2. Calisse, in Theresa Walker, "Out in the Open" (an interview with four gay teens), *Orange County (Calif.) Register*, May 13, 2002.
3. Geoffrey Winder, "GSA Network Anti-Racism Initiative Report, Summer 2001." (For more information, contact Gay-Straight Alliance Network, 160 14th Street, San Francisco, CA 94103; 415-552-4229; www.gsanetwork.org)
4. Tori DeAngelis, "A New Generation of Issues for GLBT Clients," *Monitor on Psychology* 33, no. 2 (February 2002).
5. Greg Zhovreboff, quoted in Christopher Heredia, "Older Generation Sneers at 'Queer,'" *San Francisco Chronicle,* June 24, 2001.

CHAPTER SEVEN

Who Wins and Who Loses?

Social Class and Student Identities

ELLEN BRANTLINGER

Waiting to get my hair cut a while ago, I saw a familiar-looking woman sitting across the reception area thumbing through *Vogue*. She looked about thirty-five or forty years old. I puzzled for some time before I realized that this woman who looked so much older than I remembered her was Marissa, whom I had interviewed in 1992 when she was entering her sophomore year of high school.[1] As her name was called and she walked by me on fashionable, high-heeled clog sandals, the skimpiness of her miniskirt and halter top revealed a woman who was probably five feet, ten inches tall and could not have weighed more than one hundred pounds. I recalled that a decade earlier she had been a slim but healthy-looking teenager, with a gracefully rounded face and figure. In 1992 her hair was a darker blond. She complained then that her mother would not let her bleach it; now it was streaked with light tones and framed her face in shaggy layers. It looked perfect even before her hair appointment, and her darkly tanned face was made up with great expertise. Marissa's parents were acquaintances of mine. A few years earlier I heard from them that Marissa had graduated from an MBA program and was engaged and living in another state. When I saw her at the beauty salon, I assumed that she was in town to visit her parents.

One of the things an ethnographer hates to admit—especially to herself—is that she does not particularly like certain participants in her study. I began my research with affluent adolescents after having interviewed forty youth who lived in subsidized housing. I was still numb from hearing about the poorer youths' degrading school careers and how they had been treated by teachers and by students from wealthier families. These low-income adolescents were bitter that their affluent peers monopolized the high-status activities and accelerated academic tracks in their socioeconomically mixed secondary schools. They worried about their current circumstances and bleak futures and envied the better school conditions and brighter prospects of "preps," "jocks," "good students," and "respectable kids." I had come to care about the low-income youth I interviewed. As I extended my study to include the high-income adolescents, I felt as though I were moving into enemy territory. These were the schoolmates my earlier participants had accused of humiliating them with degrading epithets and of otherwise bullying, excluding, and ostracizing them.[2]

MARISSA

Marissa epitomized my preconceptions of an elite student. She lived in the most expensive area of Hillsdale and had attended the only elementary school in town that enrolled no students poor enough to be on free lunch. Having completed her freshman year of high school at the time of our interview, Marissa was on the honors track and had been a cheerleader since middle school. During that summer interview, Marissa proudly announced that she was among only four sophomores selected to be in the prestigious swing choir. She joked that she was "really tone deaf," indicating that she was aware that she likely had been chosen because of her attractive appearance and the fact that her parents could afford the expensive show costumes and trips to contests. When discussing social groups in school, Marissa usually referred to herself and her friends as "preppies" or "jocks." When asked what others would call her, she replied, "Um, maybe an airhead," which she defined as "someone pretty, [with] good hair, good figure, nice clothes . . . interested in looks, with good taste." Marissa's friends were, in her words, "popular kids, preppies." As she explained, "We all dress the same, go to the mall, hang out at somebody's house or pool, play tennis." She added that she and the girls she spent time with "talk together all the time, but never about anything important." Expressing real feelings or talking about serious topics apparently was not permitted.

Marissa's vaguely stated post–high school plans included "going to college and getting a great job," which she defined as one with a high salary and some prestige. Her ideal goal was "to be a famous model." She had not decided on a college or a major. She later confessed that her PSAT scores were "not great—nowhere near as high as my nerd of a brother." She lamented, "I'm not anywhere near as smart. He's a brain." However, Marissa got what she called "good grades, mainly As." Chris, her older brother, excelled in science and had been offered scholarships to several prestigious universities, one of which he would attend in the fall. Marissa admitted that she had to work hard to keep her high GPA, but she still resented that her mother disciplined her to a mandatory nightly study time at home and kept track of schoolwork. This was something she did not tell peers about, because it was "not cool to study." It seems that it was best to be seen as someone who was naturally smart, which meant that you got good grades without trying or caring. Marissa conjectured that her friends probably also lied about not studying, as she gave the example that before a test her peers would say, "Oh my god! I didn't study. I know I'll fail," then feign surprise at doing well. She suspected that in talking to each other about homework, they all underreported the time they put into writing papers or completing assignments, as well as the amount of support they received from their parents.

Assessing her relationships with teachers, Marissa said, "Most like me. We get along. They know I'm a good kid." When asked if she ever got into trouble, Marissa said, "Not really. I get away with stuff because teachers trust me; they know I'm just messing around when I'm, like, a little late to class or something. Oh, sometimes they give me a dirty look when I goof off too much, like complain about the work or talk to my friends when I am supposed to be listening." Marissa implied that teachers were respectful to her (and perhaps intimidated by her) because they knew that her parents closely monitored her schooling, both what Marissa herself did in school and what teachers did. She volunteered that teachers knew of her before she got to high school because Chris had been an honor student and a championship tennis player. Marissa confidently said she had been in "the most popular freshman clique." After naming "grits" as the least popular students at her school and hypothesizing that "grits don't have cliques, I don't think," she clarified her statement:

> Grits are poor. I think they mostly live in the country. We—[quickly correcting herself] some of my friends call them hicks or rednecks. I guess most live on the Hill—that's over on the west side of town. It's the slums. Grits smoke, do drugs, dress grungy. They have those hick accents. I think they usually get bad grades. They don't like school, so I think they drop

out a lot. They don't really fit in. They are troublemakers. I don't see them much; they aren't in any of my classes.

Marissa admitted that she did not personally know any low-income students and had little contact with them: "I see them hanging around in the parking lot by the vocational wing before school. They smoke, try to look tough, and—excuse me for saying this—but the girls look slutty."

TRAVIS

In terms of home and school circumstances, Travis—someone Marissa would have called a grit—was her polar opposite. The third of four sons, Travis lived with his recently widowed mother in the same apartment in subsidized housing where he had been born seventeen years earlier.[3] His two older brothers, who he said "mostly don't have jobs," also lived at home "most of the time." During my interview with Travis, one of his brothers worked on a car in the parking lot and occasionally glanced over at us with what looked like either suspicion or derision. Travis informed me that his younger brother Jimmy, a 16-year-old, had been incarcerated in a juvenile treatment center after having been convicted on burglary and drug charges two months earlier. Several times during the interview, Travis condemned Jimmy for "getting in trouble with police" and "being stupid and getting caught," but mostly for "hurting Mom."

I had heard of the four Ramage brothers, each a year apart, well before my interview with Travis. The second oldest, Mike, was a fighter who ended up being classified emotionally handicapped due to problems with anger management and opposition to school authority. While doing special education field supervision, I had watched this bright and active youngster through the five or six years that he was placed in special education classes up until the time he dropped out of school. I knew that Child Protection Services had been involved with Mike a few years earlier when he and his mother had been severely beaten by his father, who spent some time in prison because of the incident. However, teachers mainly spoke of the four Ramage boys because they were remarkably alike in appearance—and were therefore constantly being confused with one another—and because of their amazingly good looks. Variations of Brad Pitt, these blond, brown-eyed, small youths had muscular builds and walked with a spring in their step, looking as if they had important business that they must attend to quickly, although they rarely made it to class on time, if at all.

The boys' physiques made it clear that they were athletic, and they were reputed to be bright, though mostly unmotivated to do schoolwork. Junior, the oldest, had been the best student, but even his achievement and attendance were erratic. The Ramage boys frustrated school personnel because, in spite of their talents and considerable encouragement from teachers and coaches, they never sustained an interest in their classes or school-organized sports. T-shirts with various car and motorcycle motifs communicated their real interests. They were described as leaders among their equally disengaged but somewhat more rebellious peers from the housing project. As one teacher observed, "These kids live close together, have gone to all the same schools, and are in the same classes, so they are like siblings, squabbling all the time." Friction mostly involved arguments, threats, and scuffles, but there were sometimes brawls for which they would be suspended or, if weapons were involved, expelled. Nevertheless, the Ramage boys were mostly cooperative and personable, so teachers liked them. They had a lively sense of humor, but also could be unpredictably moody and unaccountably angry. From the time each of the brothers entered middle school, they conveyed that their major objective was to turn sixteen so that they could quit school. When asked about the particulars behind his own dropping out, Travis reminisced:

> The dean was giving me a bunch of trouble. She did that with all us boys. She'd hassle me about being late, missing school—I was having problems with everything. She'd call my mom and threaten her. When I quit going for a week after my dad died, she said she'd take me to court if I wasn't there every day. My mom said I did not have to go until we got things straightened out. So she suspended me. She said I couldn't come back until I had a letter from the doctor or welfare. I never liked school anyway. It was all right at Hillview [elementary] some of the time, I guess. I did not like Downing [middle school] or high school. When I was sixteen, I stopped going. I just got tired of going.

When I asked if he had any regrets about quitting school, his prompt reply was simply, "No."

The first part of the interview took place in the family living room, where Travis, his mother, and his brother Mike sat smoking and watching a soap opera. I had introduced myself as a teacher educator interested in what teenagers thought about school and told them I might be writing about their experiences for teachers and others. At that introduction, his mother smirked and said, "Travis has plenty to say about school!" When Travis said he sort of liked elementary school and felt he was "pretty good" in math and reading, his mother interjected, "Travis got lots of As when he was at Hillview. He liked that school." Travis said middle school was "all right some of the time" and that his favorite classes were math and shop. His mother proudly pointed to a wooden clock Travis had made that was sawed into the shape of the state and painted in the local university colors. The clock hung on the wall in the middle of a cluster of school pictures, which showed her sons' cute faces representing their first-grade to early teenage years. No prom or graduation pictures were among them. Travis added that his middle school gym teacher was "nice" and "got me to wrestle." His mother then bragged, "Travis won trophies in wrestling," as she pointed to two gleaming statues on top of the television. Travis' older brother piped up, "Yeah, you was good at wrestling, right Travis?" Then he turned to me and said, "Me and Junior taught him wrestling," at which point Mike guffawed sadistically and Travis shrugged.

Shortly thereafter Travis agreed to move out to a grassy area a short distance from the housing complex to complete the interview. When outside, Travis promptly denied his mother's claims about his good grades at Hillview:

> God, I flunked first grade even, but I never was in special ed—I wasn't that dumb. I never did really like school. Me and teachers did not get along. I guess I sort of did okay until in high school, then I did terrible. All they [teachers] cared about was me being on time. The dean, she did not like me. Some girls got in a fight over me and she blamed it on me—said, "You get around, don't you!"

When I asked how long he had participated in wrestling, Travis confessed that his wrestling career was cut short in eighth grade when he was not allowed to be in extracurricular activities because of school absenteeism, tardiness, and low grades in several courses.

Although Travis asserted that "me and teachers didn't get along" and reiterated that belief in response to several questions, when asked to describe a favorite teacher, Travis responded without hesitation:

> I loved Mr. E. [his fifth-grade teacher]; he was a real cool teacher. He helped me a bunch of times when I did not understand—he cared about me. Other teachers did not care. They'd just get mad and say, "You'll flunk if you don't do your work." They didn't care what happened to me. We'd argue a lot. I wouldn't understand something and they'd say, "Well I

just showed you how to do it!" [When quoting teachers, he raised his voice and mimicked a sharp, ugly tone.] And I liked Mr. F. [his middle school gym teacher and wrestling coach]. He was nice. All the kids liked him and he liked us. We had fun in his class. Most teachers was snobby; some was all right. If you didn't understand, they didn't treat you like a piece of trash. Some teachers helped you if you had a problem. Most didn't. They helped some kids, their pets, but they didn't care about most of us, didn't care about me, if I flunked or anything.

When asked if he thought that some kinds of students had an easier time in school than others, Travis's immediate response was, "Yeah, preppies, rich kids. They got away with things. Teachers were hard on me and my friends." When asked about his relations with other students when he went to high school, Travis said:

> I had some friends—we stuck together. The punks were smart alecks—we avoided them. They would start fights and things like that. The preps ran the school. They would smart off and call us grits and stuff like that. They didn't bother me. I just kept away from them. I didn't care.

Travis emphasized "not caring" at several points in our conversation, but his animated and emotional tone belied the validity of this assertion.

Travis dropped out of school in the middle of the second semester of his freshman year when he was of legal age, sixteen years old. He admitted that he had been suspended twice in the fall for "missing class and being late" and so had not successfully completed any high school courses prior to his officially dropping out. Travis said of his mother, "[She] didn't want me to quit, but said, 'If that's what you want to do, then do it.'" He went on to explain, "She'd rather see me quit than in trouble. Besides, she let my brothers drop out, so it wouldn't be fair to make me go. Anyway, she didn't finish herself, and my dad dropped out when he was real little."

When I asked about his plans for the future, Travis said he would like to "find a job that pays good, maybe work in a factory." He said that because his father died in a quarry accident he was not interested in quarry work, adding, "That's not steady work anyway—never was for my dad." Travis was vehement that he intended to keep out of trouble and out of jail, again mentioning how upset his mother was about his younger brother's incarceration. When asked about the availability of factory jobs, he shrugged, then volunteered in a bitter tone, "Junior [his oldest brother] had a job that paid real good, but they let him go. Most of that factory moved to Mexico, so only guys with seniority got to keep jobs." According to Travis, Junior had a good salary during the approximately two years he worked and had been able to move into a mobile home he rented until he was laid off. Neither Travis nor Mike, his second-oldest brother, had found full-time employment in the year since both had dropped out of school. All three brothers had done some temporary maintenance work at a local stock-car race track and at a demolition derby site in a nearby town. Junior sometimes was called in for pick-up work at an auto mechanic shop, but this did not happen often enough for him to fully support himself and live on his own. When asked about his ideal goals, Travis said he would like to work on motorcycles or race cars—a love he and his brothers shared. Most of all, he wanted to be a race car driver.

SOCIAL-CLASS RELATIONS IN SCHOOL

Marissa and Travis were part of an interview study I did with forty low-income youths[4] and thirty-four high-income youths in the early 1990s.[5] A major finding of that study was the high degree to which the nature of adolescents' school careers correlated with their class status: Affluent students were making good grades and were on or above grade level and in advanced-track classes, whereas 35 percent of low-income participants were identified as learning disabled, emotionally handicapped, or mildly retarded and were receiving special education services. Also, 37 percent had been retained one or two years, and few of those on grade level claimed to be making decent grades.

The extent to which social-class issues permeated adolescents' stories about school and their views of themselves in the school environment was a surprise to me. Echoing the words of sociologist Philip Wexler, I "was not prepared to discover how deeply the differences of class run in the lives of high school students."[6] Social class certainly figured as prominently as gender or race in their identity construction. As illustrated by Marissa and Travis, adolescents are not passive imitators of class-distinctive ways of being; rather, they are agents that perform class-distinctive roles in innovative ways, and thus they actively contribute to the reproduction of class roles in their own social setting.[7]

When examining the schooling of youths from different social classes it would be easy to portray such students as Marissa as winners and those like Travis as losers. However, although I earlier alluded to Marissa's worrisome thinness and anxious demeanor in the beauty parlor to hint at her difficulties as a young adult, I omitted statements she made in her interview that indicated all had not been ideal in her adolescent world. First, she expressed resentment that her parents expected her to be in all the advanced classes and prestigious activities in school as well as to be popular with peers and teachers. She implied that they cared more about what others thought than how she felt. She mocked her parents' bragging about "Chris' genius" to their friends, was distressed that they thought he was more likely to succeed in an important career, and expressed worry about her own future. In spite of my reassurance that her sterling grades indicated she was smart, Marissa reiterated that those grades resulted from hard work, help from her parents and tutors, and parental intervention with teachers. She insisted that she "did not catch on easily or really understand" in all of her subjects and implied that she was an academic imposter. As she discussed being an "airhead," there were glimmers of awareness that this image allowed her to mask her feelings about many things in her life, and, because the airhead role included not being serious about anything, it also served to hide her insecurities about not being as bright and competent as others expected her to be.

Neighborhood youths who were interviewed identified Marissa as "having it all," yet she was bitter about her peer interactions. Sensing her peers' envy and readiness to unseat her, Marissa felt her clique membership was fragile. When asked about friendships, she first reeled off a few names and then recanted to say that these girls were not true friends because they were "two-faced" and she could not depend on them. As the interview progressed, Marissa emotionally poured out information about her problems in a way that suggested she had nobody to whom she could confide her feelings on a regular basis.[8]

After seeing Marissa in the beauty parlor this year, I learned that she had moved back home after resigning from her job because she felt she had been passed over for a promotion. She also had serious marital problems that remained unresolved.[9] Her mother categorized Marissa as "sort of having an emotional breakdown." When I asked Marissa's mother, Catherine, what Chris was up to, she retorted, "Good question!" She then anxiously confided that in the many years since having completed his undergraduate work he had started and dropped out of two distinguished master's degree programs. Although he had an "okay job," he was unsettled about a career and "had no steady relationship."

Apparently, Travis' fate after his immediate postschool years continued to be pulled by the difficult currents of poverty. A few years ago, I read in the local newspaper that Travis hanged himself from a tree in the park by his housing complex—probably close to the site where I had interviewed him seven years earlier. Travis was twenty-four. His obituary listed three offspring with different last names, presumably their mothers' surnames.

Occasionally I have reason to go to the neighborhood where I first interviewed Travis. I see the effects of poverty on space and people—the nature of his diminished environment is blatant. It not only offends my middle-class sensibilities, but people in the neighborhood also understand its impact. As Larry, one of Travis' neighbors, elaborated:

> This part of town is run down—trash everywhere, nobody's got money to fix things up. There's no grass, no flowers, only a few scraggly trees. In the area of town that we live in, the children are more or less pushed off. . . . The school system says you're underprivileged and your parents are failures, so you'll be failures. I'm not going to say all the faculty does. There are some teachers that go out of their way to help the kids get the tools so they don't fall into the same sorts of traps their parents did. But the majority of teachers over there feel that your parents are no good, so you're going to be no good, so why should I care. . . . If you come from a certain part of town, certain things are expected of you.

Or perhaps, as Travis seems to have believed, *little* is expected of you and little is available to you. When I asked Travis in our interview what he wanted to do over the next few years, he simply answered, "I don't know—don't know. What is there to do?"

Although there is no redemption for Travis, perhaps Marissa will recover from her struggles and find happiness with future pursuits. Marissa's breakdown, or fall from middle-class grace, may not be typical. Marissa's parents perceive it as something she will recover from and believe she will go on to reattach herself to her former ambitions. However, because they were oblivious to the generalized nature of her pain when she was an exemplary high school student, it is unlikely that they understand the depths of her alienation as a young adult or how difficult it will be for her to achieve the intimacy and self-coherence that she needs. One of the things I learned from my interviews with affluent adolescents is that, although they were often annoyingly arrogant in taking their advantages at school and their high status for granted, they were not always content with their lives. Indeed, many were anxious, tense, and unhappy regardless of their relatively high achievement and apparent social success. This is not to say that because affluent students suffer in school that they suffer to the same extent or in the same way as low-income youth; nor do I intend to imply that circumstances are the same for both groups.

The stress felt by both affluent and impoverished youth originates, to some extent, from the same source: the stratifying and alienating aspects of their schools and communities. The divisive, differentiating, and humiliating school practices offered few rewards to low-income adolescents and resulted in their being angry. They described coping with school by deliberate nonparticipation, avoidance (skipping school or missing classes), and/or minimal compliance with routines. High-income youths played the winning game, but with mixed enthusiasm and at some personal cost. They worried that they did not always live up to their own and others' expectations of them. Some seemed so driven by the need to win that they could not gauge for themselves whether winning was important.

A decade after my interviews with high- and low-income adolescents, I have come to believe that though there are many losers in the complex and troubled dynamics of social-class relations in school, there may be no true winners. It therefore seems important that educators understand how class identities are reinforced in students' performances on the high school stage and how these relations might reveal the roots of some adolescents' suffering.

CLASS IN AMERICA AND THE ROLE OF EDUCATORS

There is not a conscientious educator in the United States who would not want poor children to succeed in school in the hopes that their achievement might allow them to move out of poverty. The irony, however, is that America is a country deeply divided by class and, apparently, is becoming more so all the time. In my town, for example, each newly constructed suburb has larger, fancier houses than the last one, while at the same time more and more subsidized housing units are built for the poor. There is an underpaid working class as well as a chronically underemployed or unemployed surplus class.[10] So regardless of individual aspirations or efforts, at least a portion of American adults can be predicted not to move up from their impoverished status. Their children will be the "at-risk" students of the next generation.

In my town, conditions for the working class have worsened over the past few years. Several factories where organized labor had secured good salaries and fringe benefits closed down when their work was moved to developing countries that offer cheap labor and less stringent environmental regulations. Travis' mother, who had worked intermittently as a motel maid because of the seasonal demand for motels that is typical of a university town, had not been called back after her employer (a well-established national motel chain) found it more profitable to hire a team of cleaning and maintenance staff from Eastern Europe. (They were willing to work a 48-hour week for $2.00 an hour and expected no fringe benefits.) And although construction in the suburbs is booming, workers in that trade are imported by the truckload from south of the border.

Travis was acutely aware of the lack of job opportunities and poor working conditions; he and his brothers had been unable to find steady jobs even at minimum wage. His father had never earned enough to get the family out of the projects, and eventually he and a coworker died laboring in the quarries that harvest and carve limestone for the impressive federal buildings in our nation's capital. Travis was profoundly depressed about his own lack of work opportunities, and as far as he was concerned, nobody in school cared about the "trash from the projects." For Travis and his low-income peers, school personnel were members of the other (respectable, preppie, "to-do") class who looked down on him.

The message of an uncaring world bombarded Travis at school, and as he tried to find a place in his community, his bitterness about unfairness dominated his telling of his life story during our interview. Although Travis knew that school achievement and attainment were equated with securing employment, his appraisal that good jobs would require a college degree and that there was no way he could afford college were also correct. As far as Travis was concerned, high-income students monopolized the high-status school positions just as they would dominate life opportunities in their postschool lives. Legitimately skeptical of his own ability to break class barriers, Travis invested his interest and identity in other pursuits, which were depressingly fanciful in terms of being achievable for a young man like Travis—and he knew it. Travis was bright, healthy, attractive, articulate, and personable. He was so rational and astute that he realized that investing in school was not worth his while. He found other ways to boost his self-esteem temporarily and ease the pain connected with his class condition—ways that generally expressed anger at and resistance to school personnel and other "respectable" citizens who he felt were responsible for the conditions of his social class.

Given the dire conditions for the working and unemployed classes, as well as the vulnerable state of the middle class in our current economy, what should educators do? One thing we cannot assume is that we, as an educated class, necessarily have it right. We cannot simply preach that other classes need to get their acts together and be like us, because in some ways even we are not doing so well. As high-stakes accountability measures intensify our work, we have to ask the corporate world if more jobs with better salaries will be available to "at-risk" students who do better in school as a result of our sincere efforts. We must tell what we know about the inequities that affect a substantial number of our students to people outside of schools so that they will vote for leaders whose policies will benefit a broad range of Americans and, ultimately, the students we teach.

In her disparaging description of low-income people, Marissa did not mention structural inequities related to poverty but only personal characteristics that she felt distinguished her from her low-income schoolmates. One reason Marissa did not know about students' unequal chances was that she never crossed paths with low-income people, either in her segregated elementary schools or in tracked secondary schools—or, for that matter, anywhere else in her relatively small town. Another reason that Marissa did not know about social-class conditions and relationships was that subject matter related to the working class (e.g., the history of organized labor, the extent to which the working class is overrepresented in the risky responsibility of defending America during wars) was not part of her formal school curriculum. As Marissa gloated about the worthiness of her own class compared to others, had she been asked to analyze which social class has the most negative impact on the environment? Perhaps she had learned the various parts of government and could display her knowledge of American heroes on exams, but had she been asked to evaluate the conditions necessary to ensure a truly inclusive democracy and an equitable economic system?

In addressing what students need to know, it seems that both high- and low-income students need curriculum and texts that include the stories of ordinary working-class people as well as people who are poor. They need to learn about empathetic and brave activists who have struggled to improve the life of the oppressed. On their trips to our nation's capital (if they are fortunate enough to be able to take such trips), they must be asked to consider why war monuments dominate the Mall and why there is an absence of memorials to those who have fought to improve democracy and equity within the boundaries of our country.

Educators must be imaginative in finding ways to bridge the great divide between the social classes. The other day, a principal told me that in order to prepare students for a high-stakes exam, school personnel decided to break the sophomore class into groups of ten to twelve students, which he called "families." Every adult at the school worked with a family for two or three days preparing them for the tests, then for the several days while the tests were administered. Families took breaks and ate lunch and snacks together. Students were assigned to groups by alphabetical order, so a variety of students suddenly crossed social-class and achievement-track boundaries for the first time in their ten years of schooling. The principal confided to me how inspiring it was to see these students take a real interest in each other and treat each other respectfully. He told me that, in a relief celebration following the exams in the teachers' lounge, the main topic of conversation was the disappearance of inter-class friction. In a short period of time, these adolescents were able to recognize their common humanity and see their schoolmates as peers engaged in the common task of passing these exams so that they would not have to repeat them the next semester. Indeed, the school's aggregate test scores were several points higher than expected. As might have been predicted, however, the principal also reported that after the tests everyone returned to their previously class-segregated spaces in the school.

Regardless of the longevity of their effects, efforts like these can help to reduce the effects of social class in schools; they can also be small steps toward eliminating the deep and pernicious class divisions that persist in our society. Certainly, educators need to become powerful advocates for all of our nation's children and be vocal about the ways social-class divisions make it difficult for them to educate all children to high standards. American education is often seen as a "great equalizer," but this mission is difficult if not impossible to accomplish as long as children continue to attend school and live their daily lives under such unequal circumstances.

NOTES

1. This name is a pseudonym, as are all names of people and places in this chapter. Certain other characteristics of schools and people also have been modified to ensure anonymity.
2. Don Merten provides an astute analysis of why middle-class youngsters act this way toward each other and their lower-income counterparts in school in "The Cultural Context of Aggression: The Transition to Junior High School," *Anthropology & Education Quarterly* 25, no. 1 (1994): 29–43.
3. Her husband had died at work in a quarry accident about a year before the interview.
4. I use the term *low-income* rather than *working-class* because 78 percent of the adolescents were from single-parent homes in which only 40 percent of parents were employed. Most of these parents had part-time jobs.

5. Ellen Brantlinger, *The Politics of Social Class in Secondary Schools: Views of Affluent and Impoverished Youth* (New York: Teachers College Press, 1993).

6. Philip Wexler, *Becoming Somebody: Toward a Social Psychology of School* (London: Falmer, 1992), 8.

7. Dorothy Holland, William Lachicotte, Jr., Debra Skinner, and Carole Cain, *Identity and Agency in Cultural Worlds* (Cambridge, MA: Harvard University Press, 1998).

8. Because of the extreme unhappiness (depression) shown in the interview, I asked Marissa if I could help her find support. She was vehement that she could "handle it" and that she had just "lost it" temporarily. Confidentiality requirements prevented my intervening without her permission.

9. Marissa's parents were acquaintances of mine, but I had not seen Marissa in years. Although I suspect Marissa recognized me in the beauty parlor, she seemed to purposely turn away as she walked past me. She still may have been embarrassed by her outpouring of troubles at fifteen.

10. Barbara Ehrenreich, *Nickel and Dimed: On (Not) Getting By in America* (New York: Henry Holt, 2001).

Interview

Class and Identity in a Socioeconomically Diverse High School: A Discussion with Elaine Bessette, Joan Lowe, and Bill Quinn

Greenwich High School is a well-manicured, spacious, handsome collection of buildings set back from a wooded road in Greenwich, Connecticut. Known throughout the New York area as a wealthy suburb where multimillion-dollar mansions are graced with tennis courts, swimming pools, and stables, Greenwich in many respects lives up to its well-heeled reputation. But Greenwich is also a town of socioeconomic diversity where other housing consists of smaller homes, condominiums, apartment buildings, and even public projects. About 88 percent of the eligible youth in Greenwich attend the public high school, making it a place where the daughters and sons of lawyers, financiers, and the independently wealthy attend school alongside those of service workers, struggling recent immigrants, and families on public assistance.

Editor Michael Sadowski visited Greenwich High School to talk with school staff about the ways social-class differences affect their students' perceptions of themselves and their peers. Following are excerpts from one discussion that included Elaine Bessette, the school's headmistress, and Joan Lowe and Bill Quinn, both social workers at Greenwich High.

In what ways do you believe students' awareness of their socioeconomic status, especially in comparison to their peers, affects them at this school?

Quinn: For many kids coming into this building, especially those who come from modest or middle-class backgrounds, getting a sense of the wealth of the community and the wealth of many of the kids can be overwhelming. You can see these things just by noticing the way some of the kids dress. I think it makes it difficult for some students. It can easily make them feel that they don't belong or fit in here.

Bessette: I also think the reverse is true. Some of the wealthier students who perhaps attended more homogeneous neighborhood elementary schools hit the middle school and then the high school, and they suddenly become aware of kids who don't have what they have. I sometimes wonder what that does to their sense of self, to their concept of who they are. A student might ask one of his peers, "Where is your mom sending you during April vacation?" And the kid he's talking to has a job and is going to be working in town over vacation, whereas the other kid is going off to Cancun. Those kinds of experiences might make the wealthier student realize, "Wait a second. Maybe there is another kind of life besides what I have had all along, what the people around me have always seemed to have, and what I see on TV. There are actually people who have free or reduced-price lunch. There are actually teenagers who don't have their own cars."

Lowe: I hate to say this, but I think there are also some kids who are oblivious. They are so self-absorbed that they don't really see beyond their own wealth. They think, "This is the way I am, so this is the way it is." Then there are other kids who reject their wealth. They are embarrassed by how wealthy they are, so they downplay it—the clothes they wear, and especially the cars they drive. They could drive an expensive car and they opt not to. So it really depends on who the kid is, what their values are, and how they want to relate to other kids.

To what extent do you think the awareness of socioeconomic issues plays a part in how students group together as friends, who hangs around with whom?

Bessette: Our soccer team this year was an interesting example of that. We had kids from all over the world, from every walk of life, and from every socioeconomic group who bonded together. The parents have told me several times, "What an interesting dynamic that was." But I don't know how long-lasting their bonding experience was as they moved away from soccer to other things.

Lowe: The most interesting thing about the soccer team to me was that the carryover socially was not as profound as one might think. They were buddies on the field. There was some carryover in the student center. But as far as sustaining the friendships in their social lives, that didn't really happen.

Bessette: Right. When the kids go out into the student center, they start to gravitate toward the kids they are comfortable with or those they see as the most similar to them. Some of that may arise from social-class differences. For example, a member of a team or club might say, "Let's all go over to Jane's house." Jane lives in a very nice section of town, and everyone drives over there. Then when it comes time for Anita to have everybody to her house, maybe she lives in a very modest home and she can't throw the party that Jane can. So there is definitely an aspect of class that comes into it.

Do you also see situations in which students would like to be part of a certain social circle but they don't have the money to belong? Are there kids, for example, who are jealous and wish they could go sailing on weekends like some of their peers? To what extent have you seen or heard about situations like that?

Lowe: It is not so much about money as it is about kids wanting to be in the popular group. They don't necessarily say, "I want to be like the kids who have money." But they want to do the things that the popular kids—who are also often the wealthier kids—do. Take the prom, for example. We have students who really cannot afford to do the prom the way some of the other kids do, but they do it. They pay a lot of money for their gown. They rent a big limousine. And you just know that they don't have the money to do it. I work with kids who live in the projects and are on free lunch. Yet they spend a bundle of money on the prom because that's what everyone else is doing. But I don't have many kids saying, "I wish I were one of the wealthy kids so that I could go sailing." They look at who is in the popular group and what they're doing more than they look at economics.

In what ways do you think issues of class identity affect students academically?

Quinn: Many students come into our school and compare themselves to others who may have more means or seem to have a better life. They might be extremely successful academically, but their sense of themselves is still affected by the socioeconomic disparity they see. They say to themselves, "I may fit in here academically, but there is still a disparity between what they [the wealthier students] can do, the opportunities they have, and what *I* can do." For some of these students, school can be a negative experience they remember for a long time. Unfortunately, I've talked to several former students for whom this has been the case.

Bessette: I also think there is an achievement difference between kids who have had very rich cultural experiences and those who haven't. Some students here have been brought up to read books from an early age, as well as to go to libraries and to plays, and others have really had television as their only entertainment. Some of the reasons for these differences are cultural, but I think it also has something to do with class.

Another thing that almost all the students here get caught up in, which is largely driven by the parents who are well-heeled, is the game of reputation and status that is associated with the "name-brand" colleges. I think many kids feel that they *have* to get into Yale, or they *have* to get into Harvard, and that seeps pretty deep down into the culture of the school. Even the kids who are somewhere in the middle socioeconomically get caught up in that.

It is both a positive and a negative thing about attending a high-performing school—there is an expectation for you. This year's class did very well in terms of getting into most of the colleges where they applied. But in last year's class there was some consternation. I heard laments like, "Dad went to Yale, Mom graduated from Harvard, and Johnny didn't get into either one of those two."

How else do you see perceptions about class affecting students' expectations for their own futures?

Quinn: I think class plays a tremendous role for many of the students here in that regard. For some of our Hispanic students, for example, those who are not from wealthy families already have a sense that they are not going to make it, that they cannot be more than a custodian. Even though we may tell them about the opportunities available to them—such as the scholarships available to Hispanic students who do well in school—it is very difficult for them to overcome their expectations and to feel that they can rise above them. That is why some students are not successful in this building. They *really feel* that they cannot make it. This is not just reflective of the family of origin from which they come, but from looking at society as a whole. These kids are not stupid; they are just aware of what is going on socioeconomically. They know that most of the Spanish-speaking people here live in certain parts of town and hold certain jobs. It's very difficult for them to overcome that.

Lowe: Expectations can also affect the wealthier kids in a different way. I've known a number of great, high-achieving kids here who had altruistic goals to go out and do good things in America. Some were going to be teachers, like we are. They really wanted to make some contribution to society. Then we would hear about these students years later, and we'd find out that a lot of them had, in a sense, "sold out." One student I can think of, who was planning to be a teacher, is an investment banker now. He belongs to a country club, he wears the right shoes, he drives the right car. He is not the altruistic kid that we knew when he was eighteen years old and he was going to go out and join the Peace Corps. He got into money. I could tell you more stories like that.

So even though kids want to shrug it off from their parents and they want to be altruistic, somewhere that piece of identity is deeply ingrained. They are what they were groomed to be as little children, going to the right nursery schools and then all the way up through the right colleges. It's not that there's something wrong with students living their lives this way, but it bothers me sometimes when I think about what they could have done.

How can educators support students' positive identity development, especially those students who might not be part of the dominant social groups at school?

Bessette: I think the teachers who really acknowledge a student, not just whether he got the right answer or not, but acknowledge him for who he is, make a big difference. Such teachers don't just bring students to my office and say, "Mary has the top average in my class." They might also say something like, "Mary has a new job after school." Or, "Sandra is on the dance team. Have you ever seen her dance?" Or, "Who is your favorite writer, Jeremy?" Then Jeremy will answer, "Vonnegut," and the next thing you know we are having a discussion about Vonnegut. We want every student to feel that someone knows him or her well on a personal level. I think that helps develop a sense of self.

Quinn: To me, identity is based on many things, but two things are most important. One aspect of a student's identity is, "How do I experience *myself* given all my capacities? Am I defined by what I can do academically? What I can do athletically?" That part of them that is the center of their own experience is a major part of identity. But another major contributing factor in identity is, "Who do the people outside of me say I am? Who does my family say I am? Who does the school say I am? And what does the larger culture say I am?" For students who are minority students—whether it be economic minority students, racial or cultural minority students, sexual minority students—outside society may be giving them messages that are not supportive of their true selves. And the question we need to ask as educators is how we can begin to counteract those messages.

CHAPTER EIGHT

The Impact of Disability on Adolescent Identity

MICHAEL L. WEHMEYER

Any discussion of adolescent identity and disability must begin with an acknowledgment that, fundamentally, there is no such thing as a unitary "disability identity." Indeed, it is difficult to generalize almost anything as applying to the group referred to as "people with disabilities," due in part to the sheer number of people in this category. According to a U.S. Census Bureau report, there are 52.6 million Americans with disabilities, nearly 3.6 million of whom are between the ages of fifteen and twenty-four, a large and diverse group of young people.[1] Some are born with a disability, and their identity emerges with that "characteristic" as part of how they think about themselves and how others think about them. Others experience injuries or are identified later in childhood or adolescence and must therefore accommodate this new aspect of themselves into their still forming identities. Some disabilities are "hidden" and known only by the young people who have them and those close to them, while others are openly discernible. Some disabilities affect cognitive development and performance, while others do not.

The Individuals with Disabilities Education Act (IDEA) defines a student with a disability as "a child with mental retardation, hearing impairments (including deafness), speech or language impairments, visual impairments (including blindness), serious emotional disturbance . . . orthopedic impairments, autism, traumatic brain injury, other health impairments, or specific learning disabilities."[2] The most recent report to Congress on the implementation of the IDEA indicates that during the 1999–2000 school year just over 2.5 million students ages twelve to seventeen received special education services funded under the act, and almost 300,000 more students ages eighteen to twenty-one received such services.[3] The majority of students receiving special education services are those with cognitive disabilities, such as learning disabilities and mental retardation.

In light of the variety of disabilities that exist and the diversity of young people who have them, it is a daunting task to try to describe an identity associated with adolescent disability. Still, some experiences are nearly universal to people with disabilities and provide a way of describing the impact that disability can have on identity during adolescence. It is important for educators to understand these issues so that students with disabilities have instructional experiences that promote a healthy, positive sense of self.[4]

IDENTITY AND DISABILITY

If we define identity in the simplest and most straightforward manner, an identity is, in the words of psychologist David Moshman, "an explicit theory of oneself as a person."[5] This "theory of oneself" is derived from multiple sources, including important input from peers. Thus, one's understanding of self is derived not only from personal attributions of identity, but also from understanding others' perceptions. This metarepresentational process (thinking about how others are thinking about you) is particularly salient when one of the primary "descriptors" of oneself is "person with a disability." How disability is understood and viewed by peers and others in society is a key component of the construction of identity for young people with disabilities, and the fact that disability is associated with stigma also greatly impacts the construction of self for these youth.

It can be helpful to view the relationship between identity formation and disability through a historical lens. Since the early 1900s, disability has been associated with a variety of negative stereotypes. In the early part of the century, people with cognitive disabilities were perceived as menaces responsible for many of society's ills, including crime, pauperism, and prostitution, and people with physical disabilities were seen as subhuman ("vegetables") or as economic burdens to society. By mid-century, the stereotypes associated with disability became more charitable, but they were still stigmatizing. The return of large numbers of soldiers who had been injured and disabled during World War II led to a flurry of rehabilitation and training initiatives. Medical advances that conquered diseases linked with disability, including polio, began to move public opinion about disability away from stereotypes of menace and burden. These were replaced by perceptions of people with disabilities as objects of charity and pity. The ubiquitous poster-child images and the constant pleas to "help the retarded" or "aid the victims" of numerous diseases portrayed people with disabilities as not quite menaces or subhuman, but still not equal citizens. Many of these perceptions persist today.

It is self-evident that these kinds of stereotypical perceptions can have an impact on an adolescent's developing sense of self. For example, if one is thought by others to be a burden or in some way responsible for the problems experienced by others, one's self-worth and self-confidence, not to mention one's image of oneself as a valued person, will be adversely affected. If you are a teacher, consider the number of times you have heard adolescents teasing, harassing, or even bullying their peers using terms like *idiot, retard, moron,* or *spaz.* Clearly, these perceptions still simmer close to the surface.

The perceptions of disability associated with pity and charity are manifest in a number of ways. People with visual impairments are spoken to in loud voices with clearly (and slowly) articulated measure; adults with cerebral palsy are patted on the head by well-meaning strangers; adolescents with Down syndrome are assigned to classrooms with children with disabilities from the elementary and secondary grades.

Exacerbating the impact of all of these stereotypes and misperceptions are the expectations that arise from them. Disabled people are sometimes seen as "holy innocents" and are therefore not expected to be sexual beings, marry, or have children. "Victims" and "charity cases" are seen as worthy of being helped but unable (or maybe just unwilling) to help themselves by working. "Eternal children" will, it is assumed, never live independently. Even for students with so-called hidden disabilities, such as epilepsy or learning disabilities, these stigmatizing perceptions lower expectations and limit their options and possibilities.

New images of disability are beginning to replace these older, stigmatizing perceptions, albeit slowly. These newer conceptions frame disability as a natural part of the human experience, not separate or distinct from it, and focus on the interaction between a person's capacities and his or her social context or environment. Rather than placing an emphasis on "fixing" or "curing" the person, new perspectives on disability involve efforts to modify the environment to provide more effective supports, which will in turn enable the person with a disability to succeed despite limitations. By viewing the relationship between disabled students and their context in this way, teachers, administrators, and others who work in schools can envision ways to change aspects of learning environments in order to support the positive identity development and academic success of adolescents with disabilities.

FACTORS THAT AFFECT IDENTITY FORMATION FOR YOUTH WITH DISABILITIES

A beginning point for making positive changes in schools, however, is understanding the factors related to disability that uniquely contribute to identity formation, some of which are "internal" to the adolescent and others of which arise from the experience of living with a disability. Unfortunately, most of the factors that have been studied by researchers have shown a negative impact on identity development, including cognitive impairments, social isolation, segregation, ineffective social skills, and other problems that often affect students with disabilities.

Self-definition, self-concept, and self-image. How students think about or define themselves is critical to the development of a positive self-identity. Students who have a disability often hold self-concepts and self-perceptions that are negative because of the way disability is perceived in our society. However, the experience of disability is not *always* associated with negative self-perception. In reviewing the research on self-concept and students with learning disabilities, developmental psychologist Susan Harter concluded that there are both similarities and differences between the self-evaluation patterns of normally achieving students and special education students.[6] Other research has found that the self-concept of students with mental retardation is strongly determined by the quality of their interpersonal relationships and their personal sense of well-being.[7] A student with mental retardation who has an adequate social network and a positive sense of well-being, then, may hold a very positive self-image and have positive self-esteem, independent of the fact that she or he has mental retardation. Based on these findings, it seems clear that school environments can strongly affect these students' self-esteem and self-image.

Self-efficacy and perceptions of control. Another factor contributing to students' "theories of self" is the degree to which they perceive themselves as able to act successfully *in* and *upon* their environment. This "perceived self-efficacy" is defined by psychologist Albert Bandura as "beliefs in one's capabilities to organize and execute the courses of action required to produce given attainments."[8] Psychologist Julian Rotter defined a related concept, "locus of control," as the degree to which a person is able to perceive the contingent or causal relationships between his or her actions and outcomes that might result from them.[9]

Research examining the self-efficacy, locus of control, and outcome expectations of students with disabilities has shown that many students with cognitive disabilities hold perceptions that are not conducive to promoting autonomy and enhanced self-determination. That is, they perceive themselves as either not capable of acting on their environment, not in charge of outcomes caused by their actions, or not believing that anticipated outcomes will occur. As a result, students with disabilities may be more capable of acting successfully on their environment than it appears to teachers or others (and perhaps even themselves). Students may have more skills and knowledge than they demonstrate, yet they may not display these skills because they do not believe that it will make any difference. A student with a disability who on a number of occasions has approached a group of popular students and tried to initiate a conversation but has been rebuffed will eventually quit trying to initiate conversations because he or she believes it doesn't make a difference. This has little to do with the student's social skills, and much to do with his or her belief about efficacy and control. Other students come to believe that they cannot succeed when they try to do something, so they stop trying new or challenging things because they don't believe they can achieve them, even if that belief is not based on experience. These students will, in turn, form self-identities that are based on these negative beliefs and perceptions.

There is sufficient evidence, however, that these perceptions can be changed through intervention. For example, teachers can ensure that students with disabilities experience success in classroom tasks by using "errorless" learning strategies, "scaffolding" on students' prior knowledge, and verbalizing the links between students' contributions and the successful achievement of learning outcomes. Such learning experiences, repeated over time, will support more positive efficacy and locus of control perceptions.

Self-determination. Beliefs about control over one's life form an important component in the development of self-determination. Fundamentally, self-determination refers to the degree to which someone acts as a causal agent in his or her life; that is, they act to make things happen in their lives instead of having someone else act for them.[10] Enhanced self-determination is, theoretically, an important contributor to the process of individuation (the movement from being largely dependent on others to being largely dependent on oneself) and adolescents' movement toward autonomy. In fact, setting goals, making decisions, solving problems, and advocating for oneself are all elements of self-determined behavior and essentially describe the role of the adult in our society.

Students with disabilities are not often provided with experiences that enable them to learn to make decisions, solve problems, or set goals. Particularly with regard to students with cognitive disabilities, many parents, educators, and other adults assume that students with disabilities cannot perform these kinds of tasks. However, there are numerous examples of students with cognitive and other disabilities acquiring skills related to self-determination.[11] Moreover, research has shown that students with learning disabilities or mental retardation who are more self-determined upon graduation from high school are more likely to achieve positive adult outcomes such as competitive employment, higher wages, and greater independence.[12] As such, it is important that teachers consider ways to focus instruction on promoting self-determination both to improve outcomes and to promote more positive identity development. Some suggestions follow:

Teach students the skills and knowledge they will need to become self-determined. The educational programs of all students, not excluding students with disabilities, should promote the skills students need to:

- set personal goals
- solve problems that act as barriers to achieving these goals
- make appropriate choices based on personal preferences and interests
- participate in decisions that influence the quality of their lives
- advocate for themselves
- create action plans to achieve goals
- self-regulate and self-manage day-to-day actions

Promote active student involvement in educational planning and decision-making. Planning for special education services is an important aspect of educational programming for students with disabilities, and students can and should be active participants in such planning sessions. Students can learn goal-setting skills that enable them to develop personal objectives for learning in advance of the meeting and then have those objectives considered in the planning of their educational programs. Similarly, students can be taught basic skills for participating in meetings (such as compromise and negotiation, listening skills, and assertiveness) and be encouraged to use those skills to contribute meaningfully to the discussion. Finally, students can be taught simple skills that enable them to assume a leadership role at the meeting, such as introducing meeting participants, reviewing previous goals and progress, or identifying areas of future instructional need.

Teach students to direct their own learning. Many instructional models emphasize teacher-directed learning strategies, in which the teacher is primarily responsible for providing content information, directing student response, and guiding learning. It is important, however, also to teach students self-management strategies that enable them to direct their own learning. This can be done by teaching students skills such as self-instruction, self-monitoring, self-evaluation, and self-reinforcement that put the student in charge of instructional activities typically performed by teachers. Creative teachers can easily develop self-monitoring tools that enable students with a wide array of abilities to track progress on educational goals. These might include developing a checklist to fill out at the end of the day or class period, using graphing or charting features of word processing software, or dropping a marble in a jar upon completion of a task (and teaching the student that when the marbles reach a certain level, a larger goal has been met).

Communicate high expectations and emphasize student strengths and uniqueness. One simple yet powerful thing educators can do to promote student self-determination is to have high expectations for students and to communicate those expectations often. Students with disabilities are often all too aware of what they cannot do, and are not as aware of their unique strengths and abilities.

Create a learning community that promotes active problem-solving and choice opportunities. Students who learn to solve problems do so in classrooms that value diversity of opinion and expression and that create "safe" places for students. All students, but particularly students with disabilities, can benefit from the opportunity to provide answers to problems that might be incorrect, knowing that they will be provided the support they need to learn from their mistakes. Such learning communities often emphasize collaboration and student involvement in classroom rule-setting.

Create partnerships with parents and students to ensure meaningful involvement. While much can be done through the school to promote self-determination, unless there are parallel activities occurring in the student's home, efforts at school will not be sufficient. Parents are a student's first and longest-lasting teachers, and it is important that, from elementary through secondary education, teachers work to ensure the meaningful involvement in educational planning and decisionmaking of both parents or family members and the students themselves.

THE INTERSECTION OF DISABILITY WITH OTHER FACTORS

The experience of disability does not exist in a vacuum, and in many ways the issues pertaining to disability that teachers need to consider occur at the intersection of disability and other identity-related characteristics. Gender and race/ethnicity are particularly important, in that girls and young women with disabilities and students of color with disabilities often encounter stereotypes and biases that have a more negative impact on them than on other students with disabilities.

Gender, disability, and identity. Considering issues of gender alongside disability and identity makes an already complex situation more so. It is clear that stereotypes and biases related to gender combine with stereotypes and biases related to disability to create a "double jeopardy" for girls and women with disabilities.[13]

Though employment is primarily an aspect of life that affects adults, the special issues that face women with disabilities in the job market have strong implications for the education of adolescent girls with disabilities. The authors of a Harris Poll on the employment of people with disabilities conducted in the mid-1980s concluded that perhaps the best definition of disability in the country was "unemployed." Indicators vary across time, but it is not unusual to have unemployment rates reach 80 percent among people with disabilities. As negative as these conditions are, however, the situation is even worse for women with disabilities. In a comprehensive overview of vocational and employment outcomes for women with disabilities, educational researchers Bonnie Doren and Michael Benz found that:

- Women with disabilities are less likely to be employed than women without disabilities and men with and without disabilities.
- Women with disabilities earn substantially less than men with disabilities, and the wage gap between women and men with disabilities increases as the time since exiting high school increases.
- Women with disabilities are more likely than men with disabilities to be employed in low-status occupations, and they are less likely to be engaged in full-time or uninterrupted employment.

Although research documenting the relationship between educational experiences and these adult outcomes for women with disabilities is scarce,[14] it seems evident that the root of these problems lies in a combination of two factors: 1) the social and educational experiences available to girls with disabilities in school, and 2) societal expectations for girls with disabilities in general. Educators need to be alert to the ways that girls with disabilities are treated differently, and how the curriculum content to which they have access reflects gender stereotyping and/or differs from that offered to males. In addition, educators need to provide girls with opportunities to see themselves as capable of achieving in a wide range of careers.

Race, ethnicity, and disability. As with gender, it is likely that issues of race and ethnicity affect identity formation for students with disabilities in a variety of ways. In fact, these issues underscore the need to consider the whole child and not try to parcel her or him into discrete segments.

Although there is little data available on the combined impact of race and disability on adolescent identity formation, it is a well-established fact that students from minority groups are overrepresented in the population of students receiving special education support (and male minority students are even more heavily overrepresented). In *Racial Inequity in Special Education,* Daniel J. Losen and Gary Orfield note that, while African American students account for 16 percent of the total U.S. student population, they represent 32 percent of students in programs for students with mild mental retardation, 29 percent of those in programs for moderate mental retardation, and 24 percent of students enrolled in programs for serious emotional disturbance.[15] Similarly, Hispanic students are overrepresented in special education services. Again, there are multiple reasons for such overrepresentation, including cultural and linguistic bias in testing procedures, stereotypes related to gender and race that affect referral to special education (or, often, simply *out of* the regular education classroom), and issues pertaining to the economic availability of educationally enriching experiences.

Presumably, this overrepresentation influences identity formation in multiple ways. As with gender and disability issues, expectations for the academic performance of students of color with disabilities are affected by stereotypes and biases about disability, stereotypes and biases related to race (and sometimes language), and interactions and combinations thereof. One area of particular concern for both students of color and students with disabilities—and so particularly, perhaps, for students of color with disabilities—is the school dropout rate. A recent U.S. Department of Education press release placed the national high school graduation rate at 86.5 percent. The rate for African American students, however, is 83.7 percent, and for Hispanic students it is 64.1 percent. The dropout rate for students with disabilities ranges from 25 to 30 percent, but varies by disability category. Slightly more than one-third of students with learning disabilities drop out, while almost half of students with emotional and behavioral disabilities drop out before graduating. Similarly, nearly half of all minority students receiving special education services in urban settings drop out of school. This illustrates one of the drawbacks of being labeled as having a disability. Presumably, students who receive special education services get the individualized instructional assistance they need, but only about one-fourth of students with disabilities graduate from high school with a regular diploma.

FOSTERING SCHOOL SUCCESS

Issues affecting "disability identity" are closely tied to the contexts in which adolescents live, learn, and play. Much of the discussion about this issue (including this chapter) focuses on factors that have a negative impact on the identity formation and development of youth with disabilities. It is important, however, that educators not dwell exclusively on these negative factors but focus as well on the "whole" student. Having a disability is, after all, only one aspect of the life experience of a student with a disability. Too often, educators behave as if this one factor were the only factor to consider. Students with disabilities are more *like* all other adolescents than they are *different from* them, if one can see past the disability. Students with disabilities have the best opportunity to develop a positive, healthy identity when they are included in the educational and social contexts that other adolescents experience and are provided the supports they need to succeed in these environments.

Unfortunately, a large percentage of students with disabilities receive their educational services in settings outside the regular education classroom. According to the most recent report to Congress on the implementation of the IDEA, only 14 percent of students with mental retardation, 45 percent of students with learning disabilities, and 25 percent of students with emotional or behavioral disorders receive their education primarily in the regular classroom.

When adequate supports are available in the general education classroom (which remains an ongoing problem in many schools), it is evident that inclusive practices promote enhanced social inclusion and more positive self-concepts and self-esteem than segregated settings.[16] In a study I conducted with Kathy Kelchner, we found that that the self-perceptions of students with cognitive disabilities, as well as their perceptions of the classroom environment, differed from their nondisabled peers based on the setting in which they received their education. Students in separate classrooms perceived their classroom environment to be more controlling, thus offering fewer opportunities for exerting control themselves.

In addition to including rather than segregating students with disabilities, there are a variety of other strategies teachers can employ to promote their positive identity development. Chris Warger and Jane Burnette have identified several of these strategies as follows: [17]

Respect diverse backgrounds. Students come into learning environments with a variety of experiences. The educational process needs to take into account cultural, linguistic, racial, ethnic, and other differences in addition to disability-related variables.

Make the curriculum relevant and conducive to the success of all students. Students with disabilities can succeed in the classroom. This is not a theory but a fact. Educators who value diversity and who want to enable students with disabilities to develop a positive self-identity can do so by ensuring that all students are engaged in a curriculum that meets their needs and that promotes academic and social success.

Build on students' strengths. Perhaps the most important thing educators can do is to focus on what a student does well. Students with disabilities are very aware of their differences and their failures. Special education has, historically, been a deficit-focused process. Yet all students have strengths, and by focusing on those strengths, teachers can enable students to learn what they do well and to capitalize on that knowledge.

Provide district support to build the capacity of personnel. One frequently mentioned limitation to supporting students with disabilities is the lack of training that many educators have had to work with this population. With adequate support and ongoing training, however, all educators can provide the needed support and appropriate instruction to students with disabilities.

Adolescents with disabilities are, first and foremost, adolescents. There has been too little focus on enabling this group to develop a healthy, positive identity—one that enables them to use the skills and knowledge they have and to learn new skills and knowledge so that they can become contributing members of their communities and experience a more positive quality of life. Educators play a critical role in this process, since they can provide the instructional experiences and supports that make the difference.

NOTES

1. James McNeil, *Americans with Disabilities: Household Economic Studies* (Washington, DC: U.S. Department of Commerce, Census Bureau, 1997).
2. Individuals with Disabilities Education Act (IDEA) Amendments of 1997, PL 105-17, 20 U.S.C. §§ 1400, Sec. 602 (3)(i).
3. U.S. Department of Education, *Twenty-Third Annual Report to Congress on the Implementation of the Individuals with Disabilities Act* (Washington, DC: 2001).
4. This chapter is written from the perspective of an educator in the field of developmental disabilities. Had a person with a disability written the chapter, the focus might have been different, although it is likely that the same themes would appear. The emerging discipline of disability studies provides excellent resources for perspectives from scholars with disabilities, and readers should review Simi Linton, *Claiming Disability: Knowledge and Identity* (New York University Press, 1998) for an excellent overview of these issues.
5. David Moshman, *Adolescent Psychological Development: Rationality, Morality, and Identity* (Mahwah, NJ: Lawrence Erlbaum Associates, 1999), 78.
6. Susan Harter, Nancy R. Whitesell, and Loretta J. Junkin, "Similarities and Differences in Domain-Specific and Global Self-Evaluations of Learning-Disabled, Behaviorally Disordered, and Normally Achieving Adolescents," *American Educational Research Journal* 35, no. 4 (1998): 653–680.
7. Andrea G. Zetlin and J. L. Turner, "Salient Domains in the Self-Conception of Adults with Mental Retardation," *Mental Retardation* 26, no. 4 (1988): 219–222.
8. Albert B. Bandura, *Self-Efficacy: The Exercise of Control* (New York: W. H. Freeman, 1997), 3.
9. Julian B. Rotter, "Generalized Expectancies for Internal versus External Control of Reinforcement," *Psychological Monographs* 80, no. 1 (1966): 1–28.
10. Michael L. Wehmeyer, "Self-Determination and Mental Retardation: Assembling the Puzzle Pieces," in Harvey N. Switzky (ed.), *Personality and Motivational Differences in Persons with Mental Retardation* (Mahwah, NJ: Lawrence Erlbaum Associates, 2001), 147–198.
11. Sharon Field, James E. Martin, Robert J. Miller, Michael J. Ward, and Michael L. Wehmeyer, *A Practical Guide for Teaching Self-Determination* (Reston, VA: Council for Exceptional Children, 1998); Michael L. Wehmeyer, Martin Agran, and Carolyn Hughes, *Teaching Self-Determination to Youth with Disabilities: Basic Skills for Successful Transition* (Baltimore: Brookes, 1998).
12. Michael L. Wehmeyer and Michelle Schwartz, "Self-Determination and Positive Adult Outcomes: A Follow-Up Study of Youth with Mental Retardation or Learning Disabilities," *Exceptional Children* 63, no. 2 (1997): 245–255.

13. Harilyn Rousso and Michael L. Wehmeyer, *Double Jeopardy: Addressing Gender Equity in Special Education* (Albany: State University of New York Press, 2001).
14. Wehmeyer and Schwartz, "Self-Determination."
15. Daniel J. Losen and Gary Orfield, *Racial Inequity in Special Education* (Cambridge, MA: Harvard Education Press, 2002).
16. Gail McGregor and R. Timm Vogelsberg, *Inclusive Schooling Practices: Synthesis of the Literature That Informs Best Practices about Inclusive Schooling* (Baltimore: Brookes, 1998).
17. Cynthia Warger and Jane Burnette, "Five Strategies to Reduce Overrepresentation of Culturally and Linguistically Diverse Students in Special Education," ERIC Clearinghouse on Disabilities and Gifted Education Digest #E596 (Arlington, VA: Council for Exceptional Children, 2000). While Warner and Burnette focus specifically on the needs of culturally and linguistically diverse students, their ideas certainly warrant consideration for the education of all students with disabilities.

Profile

Making Their Own Way: The Perspectives of Three Young People with Disabilities

MICHAEL L. WEHMEYER

A discussion on disability and adolescent identity like the one presented in the previous chapter almost necessarily focuses on the challenges these youth face. Yet the stories of these three young people with different disabilities illustrate how they have learned to develop a positive sense of self, even in the face of considerable obstacles, and become ambitious, effective, self-determining individuals.

CECELIA

Cecelia Ann Pauley is a young woman with Down syndrome who speaks frequently at meetings and conferences. In a recent paper, Cecelia wrote about the importance of making her own decisions as a high school and college student:

In the eighth grade my parents asked me if I wanted to go to Churchill High School with my classmates. I said I did. The county did not want to let me go to Churchill, so we had to fight to get them to change their decision. I'm glad they did. At the end of the tenth grade, my guidance counselor asked me what courses I wanted to take the next year. I picked my classes. I liked that. I also made my own choices about what I would do after school. I was in a lot of different things, and in my junior and senior years in high school I had to choose between several different activities. For example, I was in Girl Scouts. I also was in the tennis clinic at Potomac Community Resources.

In my senior year I made a lot of decisions myself. I wanted to go with the chorus on an overnight bus trip to Orlando, Florida, to sing in a national competition. I had to save my money. I decided not to go to some movies to save enough money to pay for the trip. On this trip I decided I wanted to visit Disney World and Universal Studios with four of my friends.

During my junior year I visited several colleges. All of my friends visited colleges that year too. I visited Trinity College in Burlington, Vermont. I liked it. I decided I wanted to go there. Trinity has a neat program called Enhance for kids like me. I decided to go to Trinity. I made a smart decision.

What subjects am I taking? I had to take two life-skills courses and the freshman seminar. The other two courses I could pick. I am taking a computer course and an English course. I will take music and acting later. The two life-skills courses are "Jobs: Finding Them and Keeping Them" and "Adult Problem-Solving." My favorite class is my computer class. I can log on to the computer and send email to my family and all my friends. They all send email to me too. I love Trinity. I have a lot of friends. I like my teachers. Everyone likes me. I am learning a lot. I have a telephone in my room and I call home whenever I want. I usually call home on weekends. I decide when I want to call home.

I keep a calendar and I write in it when I am going to clean my room, do my laundry, study with my friends, watch TV, go to meetings, work, do aerobics, walk, help teachers, go shopping, go to a restaurant, and go to the fitness center. My favorite restaurants are a Chinese restaurant, a Pizza Hut, and a Ben and Jerry's ice cream store. Every day I make my own decisions. I love it.

Trinity has an alternative spring break week. Instead of going to Fort Lauderdale, Florida, on spring break, the students spend the week working with the poor. This year we can go to Washington, DC, or West Virginia. Last night we had a meeting to decide where we wanted to go. I listened to what we were going to do in both places. I decided I would go to West Virginia. In West Virginia we are going to help people repair their houses. I want to learn how to repair houses and build them.

After I graduate from Trinity I will have to decide whether I want to live in Vermont, return to Maryland, or live somewhere else. I also will have to decide what job I want and whether I want to get married. I don't know what my decisions will be, but because I make decisions now I know I will be able to make good decisions later on. All I want is a chance to make decisions about my future. Give me a chance and I will learn.[1]

JILL

Jill Allen is a young woman with cerebral palsy. She expresses her thoughts about herself and her disability through poetry, including "A Conversation with Cerebral Palsy."

> Well, cerebral palsy—
> Do you mind if I call you CP for short?—
> You've been with me for fourteen years:
> My constant companion.
>
> I accept that you are with me,
> Yet I resist you.
> I ignore you most of the time, CP.
> I hope you don't mind.
>
> Why am I,
> Of all people,
> Stuck with you?
>
> It's not fair!
> Oh, well.
> That's the way it's gotta be.
>
> I must thank you, though, CP.
> If it wasn't for you,
> I wouldn't be me.
>
> Because of you,
> I am more determined than ever
> To make something of myself:
> To succeed.

Jill reflects on her poem with the following insights:

My poem underscores two crucial points with regard to teens with disabilities taking charge of their lives. First, in order for them to be independent, they must not let their disabilities take too much control of their actions. If this happens, the teens may start to view themselves as "disabled teens" not as "teens with disabilities." Second, the teen's disability shouldn't be treated as an obstacle that has to be overcome. Instead, it should be viewed merely as something to be dealt with. If seen as something insurmountable, then the disability is always cast in a negative light. This hurts the outlook of the person with the condition. The disability needs to be viewed realistically.[2]

JOSHUA

Joshua Bailey is a young man with a learning disability. On June 4, 1997, he introduced President Clinton at the signing ceremony for the 1997 amendments to the Individuals with Disabilities Education Act (IDEA). His remarks included the following:

My fellow students here today are deeply honored to represent America's disabled students at this historic ceremony. We thank you for giving us the opportunity to get a good education and to have a bright future. I know that in years to come, we will make you very proud of us. We want you to know that we can learn, and learn just as well as anybody. All we need is the appropriate help and the chance.

I am someone who insists on having that chance. I have a learning disability called dyslexia. . . . When I entered high school, I had a discussion with one of my advisors, who said that I should take courses that I could handle easily. I looked him right in the eye and said, "No, thanks. I'll take the tough courses and do my best." And I have. Next September, when I return to school, I will take seven classes. They are Advanced Placement American History, accelerated English III, accelerated Algebra II, accelerated Chemistry, Latin III, Drafting III, and psychology/sociology. Like I said—we can learn. My advisor wasn't trying to put me down. Maybe he was being a little overprotective. Sometimes people just don't understand what we need.

As one teacher said about me, "He's the first dyslexia student I've ever taught." I think I was the first one she ever knew about. But I have found that teachers and others are willing to learn. They have good hearts and they want to help—they just need to know how. . . . Ladies and gentlemen, it is my prayer that all students—regardless of their abilities and disabilities— will have the opportunity to succeed and become contributors to this great nation. It is my great honor to introduce to you the President of the United States, Bill Clinton.[3]

NOTES

1. From "The View from the Student's Side of the Table" by Cecelia Ann Pauley, in D. J. Sands and M. L. Wehmeyer (eds.), *Making It Happen: Student Involvement in Education Planning, Decision Making and Instruction* (Baltimore: Brookes), 123–128. Copyright 1998 by Paul H. Brookes Publishing Co., Inc. Excerpts reprinted with permission.
2. From "A Conversation with Cerebral Palsy" by Jill Allen, in L. E. Powers, G. H. Singer, and J. Sowers (eds.), *On the Road to Autonomy: Promoting Self-Competence in Children and Youth with Disabilities* (Baltimore: Brookes), 93–95. Copyright 1998 by Jill Allen. Reprinted with permission.
3. Joshua Bailey, remarks, U.S. Department of Education, Office of Special Education (1997).

CHAPTER NINE

Beyond Categories

The Complex Identities of Adolescents

JOHN RAIBLE AND SONIA NIETO

What does it mean to be an adolescent in the United States today? In this chapter we attempt to provide insights into this question, based on our varied experiences with young people of different backgrounds. We are both teachers and researchers with a special interest in how race and ethnicity, social class, language, gender, sexual orientation, and other differences manifest themselves in students' identities, and in how these identities are influenced by schooling. Both of us have taught for many years at levels ranging from elementary school through university. Our research—Sonia's previous work with students of diverse cultural backgrounds and John's on-going research in "communities of adoption"—has rendered questions of identity enormously significant for both of us.[1] Our own backgrounds and developing identities are, of course, major reasons for this interest. Both John (biracial African American, adoptee and adoptive father, gay male teacher, and grandfather) and Sonia (Puerto Rican, Spanish-speaking female, teacher and teacher educator, mother, and grandmother) recognize how our own identities have shifted over the years. Hence, we share a keen curiosity about young people and the identities they create and re-create, and how their identities change based on their experiences and the contexts in which they live and study at any given time.

Human beings are constantly evolving and redefining themselves over the course of a lifetime. Adolescence is a particularly significant phase of life, during which young people try to figure out who they are. The great task of adolescence is learning to express one's multiple identities in personally meaningful and socially acceptable ways. As educators, we need to understand the implications of adolescent identity formation for schooling. How are race and gender, for instance, affirmed or dismissed in school settings? What does it mean to be a lesbian in a school setting hostile to that identity? How can an adoptee explore his identity in a school environment where biological family ties are accorded higher status than ties of adoption? And how are students' quests for meaningful identities linked to learning?

The changes one undergoes in one's identifications are due not just to individual preferences and experiences; that is, they are not simply psychological transformations that take place in one's own head. Identities also change in response to the sociopolitical contexts in which people live. Our identities have been shaped and continue to be influenced by the people with whom we interact and the material and social conditions of our lives. In this chapter, we focus on two young people who allowed us into their worlds through a series of interviews. These students come from different cities and towns, and they hail from various kinds of families and different social classes. They identify in multiple ways, based on such factors as family structure, race, sexual orientation, and national origin. In spite of these differences, they share a need to belong and to feel free to explore who they are. Finally, to explore how a sense of self can reach a comfortable—although always changing—status as one leaves adolescence, we conclude with the thoughts of a young man in the early years of adulthood.

CREATING IDENTITIES: CASES OF TWO YOUNG PEOPLE IN TRANSITION

Whether we are seasoned adults or young children, our identities are always in flux. The human impulse to categorize, however, has resulted in labeling people in ways that restrict the expression of complex identities. This tendency has been especially evident in the past several decades, given the resurgent interest in race and ethnicity in education. However, although significant in and of themselves, race, ethnicity, gender, and other traditional markers of identity do not tell the whole story.

Culture is a great deal messier than these static terms might imply. Researcher Steven Arvizu's description of culture as a verb rather than a noun begins to capture the dynamic nature of identity, particularly as defined by youth in an increasingly globalized world.[2] For instance, in their research focusing on adolescents, Shirley Brice Heath and Milbrey McLaughlin found that ethnic labels provided only partial descriptions of the young people they studied. Their research suggests that, rather than serving as a primary identifier, ethnicity gives adolescents an "additional layer of identity" they can adopt as a matter of pride.[3] In her later work, Heath found that young people, particularly those who live in urban areas, are involved in the creation of new cultural categories based on shared experiences, not just shared identities. According to Heath, these young people "think of themselves as a *who* and not a *what*" (emphasis in original).[4]

Daniel Yon is another researcher who has found that conventional, static conceptions of culture are unsatisfactory for describing the multiple and hybrid realities of identities today. Yon conducted a study of high school students of various racial and ethnic backgrounds in Toronto, Ontario. In this research, he coined the term *elusive culture* to suggest the new and creative ways students made sometimes surprising and unpredictable identifications; for instance, a Serbian student identified as "Spanish" and a White male identified most closely with his Guyanese classmates. Yon concluded:

> Youth demonstrate tremendous flexibility in their capacity to make identifications, to experiment, take risks, discard and create ideas, and in these processes they resist an understanding of culture as something to simply embody, apply, or force others to have.[5]

Raquel Romberg describes a similar phenomenon among Puerto Ricans on the U.S. mainland. *Cultural chameleons* is Romberg's term for those who "manage their lives through the combination, merging, or shifting of different cultural strategies."[6] In this way, Puerto Ricans and other young people with hybrid identities provide a far healthier model of cultural adaptation than is commonplace.

Given the pressures to assimilate to both peer culture and, in some cases, a new national culture and society, it should come as no surprise that students develop unpredictable identifications. In her ethnographic study of immigrant youth at Madison High (her pseudonym for a racially and ethnically diverse school in California), Laurie Olsen found that adapting to a new culture often meant that young people needed "to abandon the fullness of their human identities as part of the process of becoming and being American."[7] In addition, Olsen found that many newcomers were surprised that coming to the United States did not automatically make them American. For some students, especially those whose backgrounds and physical characteristics differed most from the European American mainstream culture, factors such as skin color, religion, and language prevented a facile assimulation. Students at Madison High were often forced to construct narrow boundaries for themselves, limiting possibilities of multicultural interaction. This situation was especially painful for students of biracial and multiracial backgrounds, who were often forced to "choose sides," and for many immigrants who did not fit neatly into any of the already constructed categories.

Clearly, we live in a time of transition, one in which static labels can no longer contain the rich complexity of contemporary identities. We turn now to a closer look into the lived realities of two young people who shared with us their reflections on their own unique identifications. (In what follows, the names of the young people, as well as the towns or cities where they live and the schools they attend, are pseudonyms.)

NICK GREENBERG: THE IDENTITIES OF A TRANSRACIAL ADOPTEE

Nick Greenberg is a 14-year-old middle school student. He is tall and tan, with wavy black hair and a ready smile. In physical appearance, Nick might be taken for any number of ethnicities, races, or nationalities. That is, he epitomizes a racially ambiguous individual. Nick was adopted when he was a few months old, but he maintains contact with his birth mother and his older brother, who lives with her. During this interview, Nick spoke honestly about his feelings regarding his multiracial heritage and other people's expectations for how he "should" act:

> I look more like my birth mother than my birth father because he was African American and my birth mother is White. . . . My adoptive father is Jewish, and my adoptive mother is Christian. I usually check off "African American" and "Native American" because I know I'm at least part Native American. Sometimes when I say I'm Jewish, this one kid says, "No, you're not Jewish. You have to act more Jewish." To me, I have no idea what it means to "act more Jewish." Maybe it means to wear a yarmulke or go to synagogue.
>
> I've been told that I talk White, but that was in a joking way. Certain Black kids will say I shouldn't listen to a certain kind of music since I'm Black. It kind of gets annoying to be told what music I'm supposed to listen to. They continue to press on and say I'm supposed to "act Black." When I ask them how that's supposed to be, they can't really answer that because there's no way you're supposed to act if you're Black, Chinese, White— you're just supposed to act the way you feel.

Nick identifies tastes in music and clothes, along with language styles, as important markers of identity that are frequently used to define him. Being raised by his White adoptive parents in a predominantly White environment, it is understandable why Nick "sounds White" to some. Yet partly because he listens to some rap artists, and partly because he regularly visits his birth family in a predominantly African American neighborhood of another city, Nick is able to "code-switch" and adopt an urban (some might say "Black") manner of speech. Nevertheless, it has not always been easy for him to do so.

Talking about his interactions with African American students in his middle school, Nick related a few incidents that occurred in the halls, during which he was forced to navigate tricky racial boundaries as a multiracial, racially ambiguous student. The names others hurl his way hint at their confusion about how to place Nick in the social circles at school:

> Most of the Black people act kind of racist towards me because I don't act like them. They usually say "nigger," which I find pretty offensive. Like, "Out of my way, you nigger"—stuff like that. "Nigger" is probably the worst thing I've ever been called. Some people have called me "gay." "Gay" and "nigger" are the things they call me the most. One Black person was picking on me because I didn't "act Black." And two other Black people, they kept on telling him to stop, and they said, "He doesn't have to act Black, he can act however he wants to. He can act Chinese for all I care." The first guy wasn't too happy, but he left. I thought it was pretty good.
>
> I think it's starting to sink in that people don't have to act like their race. They can act any way they want. Kids don't really have to tell anybody how they're supposed to act according to their race, or gender for that matter.

While on the surface Nick resists attempts by other students to get him to "act like his race," he nevertheless usually includes himself when he talks about Black people; that is, he identifies as African American. At other times, Nick speaks about African Americans as others. This "now I'm one thing, now I'm something else, but I'm all of me simultaneously" approach reflects a hybridized, "both/and" approach to racial identification, especially characteristic of how identifications are made by individuals who are multiracial. Such an approach is a refreshing change from the outdated "either/or" model from an earlier era, which forced people to identify with only one or the other parent's racial designation.

When asked explicitly to describe where he feels he fits, Nick answered:

I don't really choose friends by color; I choose them by who they are on the inside. I watch what they do. If they do a lot of laughing and smiling and are not acting like jerks, then I consider them nice people, and I'll see if I can make friends with them. I have a variety of friends from different races, not just a single race. I have White people, Black people, Asian people, German, Russian, Canadian, et cetera, as friends.

I don't feel I fit in with totally Black people. I feel like if it's more mixed, I have a better chance of fitting in. I would actually have to say I fit in best in the water. I know it sounds kind of weird, but that's something that I'm really good at. I can just swim around and forget about everything that's happened to me.

Nick's comment about "forgetting about everything" when he's swimming serves as a poignant reminder of the strife he experiences as a result of rigid racial categories. For him, how people act is more important than how they identify. Nick explains that he "has a better chance of fitting in" in mixed settings. Although schools sometimes respond to diversity by offering cultural clubs (such as Black student unions or Hispanic student associations), which are modeled after groups popularized on college campuses in the 1960s and 1970s, culture-specific clubs may not meet the identity needs of students like Nick. One hopeful sign is that there are more and more organizations for mixed-race students on college campuses around the country. Perhaps soon they will become established at secondary schools as well. Nick's situation further suggests that schools can do more to promote interracial activities for those who actively seek involvement in pluralistic, rather than ethnocentric, extracurricular experiences.

Elsewhere in the interview, Nick talked about visiting his birth mother and brother in the large northeastern city where they reside. Because he maintains contact with his birth family, Nick's adoption is considered an open adoption. Growing up in an open adoption has provided Nick with access to people who can answer many of the identity questions with which adoptees often grapple: Why was I adopted? Where did I come from? What does my biological family look like? Nick talked about how he handles being adopted and other people's curiosity about his unique family:

When people find out I'm adopted, they usually say, "You're adopted?" They are kind of shocked, because they thought that I was just—that they were my "real" parents and I just had a little bit darker skin.

I go to this group where everybody there is adopted. It meets maybe once or twice a month, maybe a little more. We do social activities, but we always talk about adoption and what our lives are like and how we feel about it. It kind of feels useful to be able to get it out and tell other adoptees what it's like, like children your age. We like the stuff we do, but we also like being able to talk to each other really well.

Nick's reference to people who wonder about his "real" parents indicates a common mistake made by well-intentioned individuals when discussing adoption. Some adoptees insist that the parents who raised them are their real parents, while others reject the term altogether. It is more appropriate to be specific and to talk about "birth" (or "biological") and "adoptive" parents, since all of them, whether they are known or not by the adoptee, are real people with real identities. Moreover, all have a real influence in the life of the adopted adolescent.

As an adoptee, Nick is fortunate to be able to integrate two powerful influences that shape his identity: namely, his birth family and his adoptive family. While open adoptions are becoming more commonplace, most adoptees are faced with knowing little, if anything, about their biological family origins. Discriminatory laws remain on the books and continue to deny teenagers knowledge about their birth parents, medical histories, possible siblings, and so on, until they reach the age of eighteen. At this age of majority, state laws usually allow adoptees to request access to their records, but even then information may be withheld, if it is available at all.

Nick's case is remarkably different. Because Nick's is a transracial adoption, when people see him with his adoptive parents it quickly becomes obvious that he is adopted. Furthermore, since he knows his birth mother and brother, should he ever decide he wants to meet his birth father, he can always ask them for his name and whereabouts. The open nature of Nick's adoption circumvents the problem of access to identity information; it is not restricted by outdated laws that privilege the rights of parents over those of adopted young people.

Whether adoptions are done in the innovative open manner or follow the traditional closed approach, the presence of adoptees in school raises questions for teachers who may inadvertently send biased messages to students and families. Schools help to maintain the higher status of families connected biologically by reproducing mainstream definitions of family. For instance, a school form that asks simply for "mother's name" and "father's name" dishonors the reality of the multiple parents in a complex family configuration like Nick's. Similarly, students and parents should be able to check or write in more than one category if authorities insist on asking students to identify themselves by racial group.

In addition, assignments to chart family trees in social studies or biology classes typically privilege biological ancestors and descendants, making it difficult for adoptees to participate fully. For adoptees who do have relevant information, fitting it all into the traditional linear family tree model poses a challenge. Quite simply, their huge family tree diagrams would look more like forests. For adoptees who don't have access to their birth families' histories, having to fill in the tree chart as if they were not adopted can feel dishonest at best and like a betrayal of family ties at worst. Moreover, adopted young people are often keenly aware of the contingent nature of their identities, as reflected in various family ties, family names, legal documents such as birth certificates (which in their case have already been falsified or "amended"), and other identity markers most people take for granted. Simply to appear more inclusive, if not to become more affirming of the array of student identities, schools can change to accommodate the reality of complex families that have been formed through adoption or otherwise.

REBECCA FLORENTINA: COMING OUT SAFELY
IN HIGH SCHOOL

Rebecca Florentina is seventeen years old and attends public school in the small New England city of West Blueridge, which has a visible and active lesbian, gay, bisexual, and transgender (LGBT) community. Recently, as a senior in high school, Rebecca "came out"; that is, she began acknowledging her homosexuality openly. Rebecca wears her hair boyishly short and dyed green, and a string of multicolored pride rings hangs around her neck. During the interview she wore a T-shirt that read, "I'm not a dyke, but my girlfriend is." Rebecca belongs to the school's gay-straight alliance (GSA), one of a growing number of school-sanctioned clubs that provide a sense of safety and support to LGBT students and their allies. She describes the level of tolerance of homosexuality in her community and school:

> When I came out, my friends were awesome. I didn't lose a single one. So it was pretty cool. I think, in West Blueridge, if you don't approve of the lifestyle, you don't say it, because you're going to be offending a heck of a lot of people. There are so many lesbians around. I think if people do mind, they keep their mouths shut. I just think that because we're in West

Blueridge we get treated so much better than people in other schools. I mean, people have gotten killed. You know the school is accepting because the school has a gay-straight alliance. I'm in the school's GSA. We've gone around and asked teachers to put Safe Zone stickers on their door. The majority of them actually have them on their doors. Most of the teachers don't mind. There's a couple that are kind of iffy.

There are probably three of us who are "out" at school. I walk around wearing this shirt: "I'm not a dyke, but my girlfriend is." I'm lesbian, butch lesbian, whatever you want to call it. I just want people to know that I'm not a little femmie. That's basically how I define myself.

Rebecca identifies herself not simply as a lesbian student. It is important to her that people recognize her as a particular kind of lesbian, an out, butch lesbian (or, in her words, "not a little femmie").

As an openly gay student, Rebecca has taken advantage of the GSA offered at her school. There she has found allies who share her interest in increasing the visibility of LGBT issues and in promoting a more tolerant atmosphere. But other comments Rebecca makes suggest that not all spaces in the school make her feel equally safe to express aspects of her identity:

I'm in music, and everybody there knows about me and my girlfriend, because we're both in music. They're all cool with it. And if they're not, they don't say anything. But I'll be reluctant—like I wear my sweatshirt [over the T-shirt] all the time, but I'll be reluctant to wear this in the halls, or in the bathroom or something. I don't wear this T-shirt when I'm alone in school. I don't think teachers could do anything. You're not going to stop the kids from doing something they want to do. If I'm in the hall and some other kid is in the hall, and there's no teachers around, he can hit me if he wants. Or she.

Clothing arises as an important marker of identity in Rebecca's story. She talks about her desire to increase lesbian visibility within the school by wearing her "dyke" T-shirt. At the same time, she worries about other people's reactions and threats to her physical safety. In some schools, dress codes prohibit students from wearing T-shirts that might be considered offensive, or that contain a message that might distract students from learning. Rebecca's T-shirt, no doubt, would present a challenge for teachers and administrators in charge of enforcing dress codes in such schools. It is worth bearing in mind the important role that freedom of expression plays in adolescent identity, particularly for students like Rebecca. Being able to decide where and when to display her T-shirt serves a significant function in Rebecca's exploration of her newfound identity as an out lesbian.

Rebecca's fears for her safety came up at numerous times in the interview, as well as her belief that teachers play an important role in the extent to which she feels free to express who she is:

> This girl said, "Oh, you faggot" in one of my classes, but I don't know if the teacher heard or not. Students just say "faggot" all the time. It makes me angry. I mean, there's nothing you can do, really. It made me feel so much safer when I had a teacher say, in his class the first day, "There will be no swearing, there will be no slurs like 'faggot' or whatever in my class." I have had only two teachers in four years of high school that have ever said something like that. I think if you had to hold your tongue in class without saying that stuff, it would help a little bit.
>
> When you get out in the halls, it's a totally different atmosphere. People act basically the opposite of how they act in class. The climate is like, if you're generally like everybody else, you're fine. But if you're totally opposite of what everybody else looks like and acts like, you'll get shoved into a locker or something, or told to shut up. All we can do is hope to educate teachers, because there's kids in middle school getting beat up in the hallways because of homophobia, and the teachers don't do anything about it.

Even when teachers make it a point to set standards for respectful interaction in their individual classrooms, there is often a discrepancy, as Rebecca points out, between students' behavior in class and their actions in common areas, such as the school hallways, cafeteria, library, or restrooms. This discrepancy may reflect the need for some students to gain a sense of control over the ways their identities are being constructed by their schooling experience. For example, one common way adolescent identities get expressed is through resistance to adult norms. If teachers simply impose what may seem like superficial "political correctness" about the use of slurs and put-downs, then students may well reject these values when teachers are out of sight and out of earshot.

Similarly, Rebecca's remarks about the messages students receive from school curricula are particularly insightful:

> The health class in the high school looks at same-sex whatever, or queer whatever, in a derogatory way. The curriculum says, "Here's these lesbian people, and we should accept them," something like that. It's not like, "Here's the great things about being gay." It's like, "Here's all the things that happen, and things that people think of them." And I don't even think

it's that accepting. It's just like, "There are people who are gay." And that's the whole curriculum. And, "Here's a dental dam," and that's it. And the whole class would laugh, and they'd move on. So I think if you want to educate people better, get the health teachers to put better curriculum for teaching about same-sex, transgender, anything. Because it's looked at in a negative way instead of in a positive way.

Rebecca articulates the limits of supposedly inclusive health lessons, which do make mention of lesbians, but then don't provide students with accurate, possibly controversial information about real lesbian lives and gay-related health issues. Merely mentioning a dental dam in the context of a lesson on safer sex, for instance, only gives students something to snicker about, rather than increasing their understanding of lifesaving health concerns. Clearly, teachers need assistance not only with gathering appropriate resources, but also with fashioning their own personal approaches to presenting issues that may make themselves or their students—not to mention parents or administrators—uncomfortable. By glossing over and oversimplifying LGBT issues in the way Rebecca describes, teachers reinforce simplistic labeling that can restrict the lives of LGBT students.

Rebecca sums up her assessment of how much teachers at her school support her lesbian identity as follows:

We have an English teacher who has a lesbian daughter. That's the only reason he brings stuff up like that. Now he's talking about gay issues, like every other day in class. He doesn't talk about his daughter, but he's letting the kids read books that are very liberal and very queer-friendly. I think the teachers who are like that are the teachers who have a lesbian daughter, or are gay themselves, or who have the kids in class saying, "I'm a lesbian. You're offending me in class, like me and my other friends." That's the only reason they do it.

Lesbians are just like everybody else. I mean, everybody sees it as somebody who's different and not normal. But it's just your sexuality. I don't identify myself as like, "Hi, I'm Rebecca and I'm a lesbian." It's like, "This is me, and this is my sexuality." That's as far as I'm going to go with it. I mean, I'll wear a T-shirt or something—I'm proud of who I am. But by wearing this T-shirt, all I'm saying is that here's a happy kid, I'm fine, whatever.

Teachers should value open-mindedness, I think, and being inclusive of everybody. It's hard to be politically correct in everything, every second in every word you say. But I don't know. There are some teachers you just don't want to approach sometimes, because they are very closed.

We cannot overstate the significant role played by the teacher in establishing the climate in the classroom. Even when teachers attempt to share power and run their classes in a democratic fashion, students may still see the classroom as belonging to the adult authority figure. Rebecca placed as much responsibility on her teachers as she took herself. For example, she expresses appreciation for the teachers who make an effort to use inclusive language, who set class expectations for tolerance, and who bring gay content into their lessons. At the same time, she doesn't wait for the world to change before she herself takes action. In the way she negotiates the expression of her unfolding lesbian identity, Rebecca is an inspiring example of the power of one individual to make a difference, simply by insisting on being true to herself.

IMPLICATIONS OF COMPLEX IDENTITIES FOR EDUCATIONAL PRACTICE

While identity construction might appear to be a profoundly personal matter, it is also a social and political matter, precisely because it is deeply implicated in the struggle to develop a sense of self within a social sphere. Thus, these are not just individual issues; rather, they have implications for educational practice, as well as for the social and cultural climate created in schools. These implications relate to teachers' professional development as well as school policy and practices. For educators who choose to provide a safe space for the free exploration of adolescent identities in schools, a number of important lessons can be drawn from the students' experiences presented in this chapter.

The themes of choice and flexibility are crucial for youth. Because their identities are in flux and more complicated than static labels can hope to convey, neither of the young people featured here would appreciate being labeled permanently with any one descriptor. For example, Rebecca is not simply a lesbian; she wants to be known as a butch lesbian, and not a "femmie." Furthermore, at the same time she makes visible her lesbian identity and advocates for its equality with other identities, she insists that she is more than her sexuality. She also identifies as Italian and as a musician, for example. Similarly, Nick is African American, European American, Native American, Jewish, and Christian simultaneously. He is also part of and loved by the members of both his birth family and his adoptive family, all of whom are real family to him. Schools need to catch up to the fast-changing identifications being created and re-created as today's students make their way through complicated social contexts.

Opportunities for peer association are valuable to students, in class and out. In their own ways, Nick and Rebecca articulate the benefits they gain from speaking with other young people who share similar situations. For example, Nick discussed the importance of his adoptees' group, and Rebecca mentioned the meaning she finds as an active member of the GSA. Although none existed at her school, Rebecca mentioned that she would join an Italian American cultural club, were one available; similarly, Nick might benefit from participating in a multicultural interest group, particularly one organized specifically for multiracial students.

While both students expressed the opinion that "teachers can't really do anything" about harassment in school, it is nonetheless incumbent upon educators to create school environments that are free from bullying. Teachers can do more to share power with students in order to develop school climates that genuinely respect diversity. Specifically, teachers can work with students in ways that go further than forcing them to pay lip service to politically correct verbiage only when adults are around.

How do teachers invite students to co-create respectful school climates? Rebecca's case suggests that modeling behavior that takes LGBT concerns seriously is one place to start. Elsewhere in her interview, Rebecca talked about a teacher who commented casually at the end of class that he had seen an article in the newspaper about a gay issue. Rebecca described feeling accepted and affirmed when he unexpectedly brought up a topic of concern to her as a lesbian. Having such conversations publicly, within earshot of other students, sends a clear message that LGBT topics are not taboo. Moreover, students learn that gay issues can be discussed seriously by gays and straights alike.

Teachers need more time to focus on issues of identity and diversity, both through their preservice education and through inservice professional development. Although schools and colleges of education are devoting more attention to concerns of diversity and identity, there is still much work to be done. Teachers who are planning curricula around themes of family heritage, genetics, or genealogy, for example, might benefit from professional time set aside to think through the implications of their lesson plans for marginalized groups, such as adopted, bicultural, or LGBT youth. Using curricula to reflect the realities of nontraditional families, such as those headed by two lesbian moms, for example, as well as families formed through adoption, invites all students to feel freer to express their unique identities in a climate of openness, safety, and mutual respect. Finally, providing teachers with time to reflect on and reconsider their own ideas about race and ethnicity, sexual orientation, and changing definitions of family can help schools become more affirming of the complex identities of today's students.

JOAQUÍN ROSARIO: BEGINNING ADULTHOOD WITH A STRONG SENSE OF SELF

We conclude our exploration of adolescent identity with the words of a man in the next stage of his life, young adulthood. Joaquín Rosario is twenty-two years old, and he currently attends one of the most prestigious liberal arts colleges in the nation. He grew up in poverty in a large urban area where he attended public schools, excelling so much that he received a full scholarship to the college. Joaquín confessed that in high school he had the "freedom" to excel academically because, besides being a strong student, he was an accomplished athlete. This identity gave him tremendous credibility in the eyes of his peers. But claiming his identity as both an urban Puerto Rican and a good student was not always easy. How could he be both in a context that only valued one or the other?

Joaquín noticed at the college's orientation that he was one of only two Latinos in the entering class. In spite of this context, it took going to a college steeped in privilege for Joaquín to be given the opportunity to study his heritage. It was after this experience that he began the process of claiming both identities of Puerto Rican and scholar, and along the way he picked up even more ways to define himself. Thus, Joaquín has emerged with a strong sense of self, comfortable with the complexity of his identity. And although he is "only" Puerto Rican, Joaquín recognizes that even what may seem to be a fairly straightforward identity is more complicated than it may appear. He says he can neither "limit his identity" nor define it solely in terms of his ancestral homeland. While he feels connected to the island of Puerto Rico through family stories and through cultural traits such as language, music, food, and clothing, to name a few, Joaquín remarks that his identity is always more complex than "just one thing." Here are his thoughts about who he is and how he arrived at this point:

> Physically, I can only trace my roots as far back as my great-grandparents. One of my great-grandmothers is still alive. She's ninety-eight years old and can still remember how she had to fetch water from the well, and how

her house was made of wooden planks and sheets of aluminum with a dirt floor. Historically, however, I am aware that as a Puerto Rican I come from a long history of merging and mixing of bloods and cultures. The indigenous inhabitants of the island now called Puerto Rico; the European traders, conquistadors, and slave owners; the African slaves (who were a diverse group to begin with) that were brought to the island both to work and be traded, are all ingredients of who I am.

But I cannot limit my identity to the history of the island where all four of my grandparents were born. Being born and raised in the urban center of a Northeast city, many more things have been factors in molding my life and my identity. I am an urban, bilingual, heterosexual, Roman Catholic, Puerto Rican male that enjoys listening to salsa as much as hip-hop, who can savor the taste of *tostones* as much as a side of collard greens. I can wear baggy jeans, a "hoodie," and "Timbs," put on a three-piece suit with high polished shoes, or a *guayabera* and Dockers, and fit in anywhere I go.

My multiple cultures allow me to move seamlessly across borders. I can speak proper English with an almost undetectable accent, I can talk as much trash about "yo momma" as anyone else in my neighborhood, or I can drop some knowledge while spitting/speaking my Spanish/Spanglish slang. My identity cannot be classified or contained into one or two categories. I am always much more than just one thing.

It is clear that border-crossing for Joaquín is not simply a metaphor, but an expression of his lived reality. Joaquín can and does move literally across boundaries marking different neighborhoods and even nations, as well as different social contexts and linguistic communities. This mobility leads to the hybridity, adaptability, and freedom of choice he enjoys.

LEARNING FROM YOUNG PEOPLE WITH COMPLEX IDENTITIES

Unfortunately, not all young people have the privileges that Joaquín enjoys. As elementary and high schools move to affirm students in their identity explorations, students will have fewer reasons to struggle through adolescence in silence and confusion before claiming their selfhood. It is imperative that all educators understand how race, gender, and other differences matter in school. Many teachers, particularly those at the secondary level, would rather focus on the content they teach than on the emotional and social concerns of their students. But it is becoming more obvious that these cannot be separated.

In her research at Madison High, Laurie Olsen found that the great majority of teachers did not believe that they needed additional preparation to serve the new diversity at the school. Most reported that being "color blind" was enough. Yet Olsen's research revealed tremendous discordance and rage among the students in the school, as well as a silence concerning racism and other forms of exclusion.[8] This underscores the need for teachers to come to grips with what impact identity has on students' learning and their sense of belonging at school.

For students who do not fit into tidy identity boxes, raising teachers' awareness of changing identifications among adolescents can enhance this sense of belonging. In our interviews with students who negotiate complex identities on a daily basis, they expressed a need for teachers to take notice of intolerance based on identities rendered invisible by the school. Both Nick and Rebecca spoke poignantly of the impact of harassment in the hallways, and even in classrooms, about which teachers apparently knew and did nothing.

The task of supporting the complex identities of students like Nick and Rebecca is as complex as these students are themselves. Yet as researcher Frederick Erickson has written, "When we think of culture and social identity in more fluid terms . . . we can find a foundation for educational practice that is transformative."[9] How can teachers and other educators engage in the kind of transformative practices that Erickson suggests? One way might be to envision multicultural school communities as "cultures of commitment" (to borrow a term from anthropologist Gerd Baumann).[10] These are associations of diverse individuals that cut across national, religious, ethnic, and other identifications but are united by a common purpose, a shared project and vision.

If educators, for example, united their school communities around a vision of high expectations and democratic participation for all students, schools might more effectively foster inclusive, respectful, accepting, and empowering school climates. In such environments, perhaps more students would find the freedom to explore their unfolding identities and form new identifications based not on outmoded, confining labels, but on their real needs.

NOTES

1. Sonia Nieto, *Affirming Diversity: The Sociopolitical Context of Multicultural Education*, 3rd ed. (New York: Longman, 2000); Sonia Nieto, "Lessons from Students on Creating a Chance to Dream," *Harvard Educational Review* 64, no. 4 (Winter 1994): 392–426; John Raible, "Re/Constructing Race: An Ethnography of Trans-

racial Adoption," paper presented at the conference of Ethnography and Qualitative Research in Education, Pittsburgh, June 2002.

2. Steven F. Arvizu, "Building Bridges for the Future: Anthropological Contributions to Diversity and Classroom Practice," in Robert A. DeVillar, Christian J. Faltis, and James Cummins (eds.), *Cultural Diversity in Schools: From Rhetoric to Reality* (Albany: State University of New York Press, 1994), 75.

3. Shirley Brice Heath and Milbrey McLaughlin (eds.), *Identity and Inner-City Youth: Beyond Ethnicity and Gender* (New York: Teachers College Press, 1993), 222.

4. Shirley Brice Heath, "Race, Ethnicity, and the Defiance of Categories," in Willis D. Hawley and Anthony W. Jackson (eds.), *Toward a Common Destiny: Improving Race and Ethnic Relations in America* (San Francisco: Jossey-Bass, 1995), 45.

5. Daniel A. Yon, "Urban Portraits of Identity: On the Problem of Knowing Culture and Identity in Intercultural Studies," *Journal of Intercultural Studies* 21, no. 2 (2000): 143.

6. Raquel Romberg, "Saints in the Barrio: Shifting, Hybrid, and Bicultural Practices in a Puerto Rican Community," *MultiCultural Review* 5, no. 2 (1996): 16–25.

7. Laurie Olsen, *Made in America: Immigrant Students in Our Public Schools* (New York: New Press, 1997), 239.

8. Olsen, *Made in America*.

9. Frederick Erickson, "Culture, Politics, and Educational Practice," *Educational Foundations* 4, no. 2 (1990): 22.

10. Gerd Baumann, *The Multicultural Riddle: Rethinking National, Ethnic, and Religious Identities* (New York: Routledge, 1999), 153.

From Understanding to Action

MICHAEL SADOWSKI

Throughout *Adolescents at School*, the contributors have drawn on the voices and experiences of young people to illustrate many facets of identity in vivid, real terms. Broadening and deepening readers' understanding of this complex set of issues has been a primary objective of the book. But in the enterprise of American education, where real students enter real schools every day, a mere academic understanding is not enough. Thus, the second purpose of this book has been to provide educators with ideas for action: ways they can work with students to help put them on a course toward higher achievement and better lives.

With this purpose in mind, many of the authors herein have provided practical recommendations that outline how educators and school communities can work toward a variety of goals. Pedro Noguera's recommendation to assign student groups to avoid self-segregation and Ellen Brantlinger's call for lessons that expand students' understanding about the contributions of poor and working-class Americans are two such examples. There are also a number of larger "lessons" that emerge from these chapters as a whole, six of which are identified here. These lessons suggest ways that all educators can begin to work more effectively with the adolescents they serve.

1. Listen to students. Perhaps the most recurrent theme among these chapters has to do with the importance of listening: hearing what students themselves have to say about who they are, how they see themselves in the school environment, and what they believe is expected of them as learners. The students who participated in the Fort Wayne workshops (highlighted in Thomas Fowler-Finn's piece) probably taught educators more about how to close the Black/White achievement gap than did any of their analyses of test scores, dropout statistics, or other quantitative data. Similarly, the three students profiled in Michael Wehmeyer's "Making Their Own Way" reveal much about how students with disabilities might view themselves, their disabilities, and their learning. While we certainly cannot make assumptions about all students of color or all students with disabilities based on profiles like these, they remind us nevertheless that students are at the core of our work and may hold more of the answers to their own success than we realize. Creating opportunities to listen to our students may well be a crucial element in any effort to raise achievement.

2. Make no excuses, but ask a lot of questions. Under accountability-based reform, urban schools serving large percentages of poor children, who are often disproportionately students of color, are held to many of the same achievement standards as schools in higher-income areas. This is often called the "make no excuses" approach to improving education for low-income students. Poverty, racism, and other institutional factors are, in a sense, discounted, based on the assumption that such excuses only perpetuate inequities by encouraging separate standards for children living under more difficult circumstances.

While it may be true that lower standards serve no students well—least of all those for whom education may be one of the few tickets out of tough socioeconomic conditions—it is still important to ask *why* a large number of these young people do not succeed academically. If, as Noguera notes, students of color are responding in some way to peer influences or perceptions that they have fewer opportunities than their White counterparts, it is important for educators to explore these factors, even while they hold a uniformly high bar for achievement.

For very different reasons, Michael Kimmel calls on us to ask the right questions rather than accept mere excuses about school violence, such as the facile explanation that it is simply the result of media violence and therefore requires no examination of our culture or our schools. And Michelle Galley encourages us not simply to accept the "fact" that girls do better in courses requiring verbal ability and boys do better in math and science. Galley suggests that we consider *why* such conditions exist, *how* the work of educators supports these conditions, and *what* teachers can do to support boys and girls as learners simultaneously.

3. Be willing to take risks. Beverly Daniel Tatum observes in her commentary that opening the conversation about race can seem like risky business in many school cultures. Yet, only by starting this dialogue can educators begin to understand—and break down—some of the barriers to school success that disproportionately affect students of color. Similarly, as I note in my own chapter, engaging in an honest assessment of the ways a school's environment affects lesbian, gay, bisexual, and transgender (LGBT) students is a difficult and often painful task. Taking action to improve the school climate for LGBT students can be even tougher, given the opposition that can arise in response to such measures. Ethnicity, ability, gender, social class—none of these is an easy topic to grapple with in a school community, but taking the risk to deal with these issues frankly and productively is necessary if we truly aim to serve all students well.

4. Rethink the curriculum. Stacey Lee, Ellen Brantlinger, and other authors in this book suggest that teaching in a way that is responsive to the identities of all students requires rethinking what topics are represented in the curriculum. Although revising curriculum to represent diverse identities might be dismissed by some as "politically correct," it is important to remember that no curriculum is identity neutral. Curriculum as it has traditionally been developed reflects choices about which aspects of American identities are widely represented and which are not. While much of this reflects centuries of our history and embedded cultural conditions that will not change overnight, we should at the very least be asking whether our curriculum reflects the identities of *all* the students in our schools as much as is practical. As Arthur Lipkin has aptly said about curriculum, "expurgation is dishonesty," yet such exclusion is often the rule in the slowly changing culture of schools.

5. Challenge yourself and your assumptions. Considering aspects of identity also means taking a look at ourselves: who we are, the experiences we've had, and the belief systems we've acquired along the way. For example, are we influenced in any way by the model minority or perpetual foreigner stereotypes about which Lee writes? Do we, as Angela Valenzuela suggests, subconsciously label immigrant students as less capable, not "honors material"? Do we assume that all families are based on the traditional model, or that all students who belong to a certain group experience their identities in a similar way? As products of our culture, we are all susceptible to stereotypes, assumptions, expectations, and prejudices that affect the way we see adolescents. Facing and challenging these assumptions—and perhaps questioning our own identities in the process—is an important step toward approaching our work in ways that reflect a better understanding of our students.

6. Offer diverse opportunities for students to succeed. Serving the wide diversity of students in our schools means making our schools more diverse. This does not mean returning to the model of the "shopping mall" middle or high school or abandoning a focus on core curriculum. But if we are, as Michael Nakkula suggests, to provide multiple opportunities for young people to invest psychic energy and explore diverse possibilities for themselves, then a "one-size-fits-all" approach to schooling will not suffice. We need to be willing to consider a wide range of curricular and extracurricular options—everything from mentoring programs to heterogeneous grouping to afterschool clubs for multiracial students—if we wish to encourage students' investment in school and their achievement. And, as Brantlinger and others suggest, it is critical that we encourage all students—not just those with the most social or intellectual "capital"—to take full advantage of what school has to offer them.

Amid the fast-paced, day-to-day world of schools, it is all too easy to lose sight of the fact that adolescents are what middle and high school education is all about. Getting to know more about this primary constituency, in all its fascinating complexity, is not a frivolous detour from a hard-driving focus on academic performance; rather, it is a crucial aspect of the work of educators, one that perhaps has a greater bearing on school performance than any other. Our hope is that this book has supported reflection, understanding, and action toward the goal of improving adolescents' achievement, as well as their lives.

Acknowledgments

The publication of this book has largely been made possible by the William T. Grant Foundation, to which I am grateful not only for its generous financial support but also for its unfailing commitment to improving the lives of children and youth.

I also owe tremendous gratitude to each of the contributors, whose important work is reflected in these pages; to Douglas Clayton, director of the Harvard Education Press, for believing in this project and guiding it toward completion; to David Gordon, editor of the *Harvard Education Letter*, for his valuable advice on the structure of the book and for his expert editorial eye; to Dody Riggs, HEP production manager, and Karen Walsh, marketing director, whose creative ideas were a frequent source of inspiration; to *Harvard Education Letter* board members Laura Cooper, Peggy Kemp, and Milli Pierce, for their thoughtful input in helping me conceptualize the book; to Laura Clos, HEP staff assistant, for handling the details with skill and good cheer; to Harvard Education Press staff members Alice Carter, Wendy McConnell, Marilyn Lofaro O'Neill, and Meg Wilson for their inspiring enthusiasm about the book; and to my partner, Robb Fessler, for his tremendous support throughout the process.

This book is dedicated to all of the young people whose voices are heard throughout these chapters. Their willingness to tell their stories will help teachers, counselors, and administrators serve other young people better.

About the Contributors

Darcia Harris Bowman is a staff writer for *Education Week*, based in Washington, DC, where she writes about school security and health issues for a national readership that includes school administrators, state and federal policymakers, and teachers. Since joining the newspaper in January 2000, Bowman has also covered charter schools and vouchers, reported on education policy in Arizona and Minnesota, contributed to coverage of the aftermath of September 11th, and provided follow-up reporting on several school shootings.

Ellen Brantlinger is professor of curriculum and instruction at Indiana University. She has written extensively on the issues surrounding social class and education, as well as other education-related topics. She is the author of *Dividing Classes: How the Middle Class Negotiates and Rationalizes School Advantage* (Routledge/Farmer, 2003), *Fighting for Darla: A Case Study of a Pregnant Adolescent with Autism* (Teachers College Press, 1994, with Susan Klein and Samuel Guskin), and *The Politics of Social Class in Secondary School: Views of Affluent and Impoverished Youth* (Teachers College Press, 1993). Her writing also has appeared in numerous edited books and journals, such as *Sociology of Education, Anthropology and Education*, and the *Journal of Adolescent Research*.

Theresa Squires Collins teaches English at Evanston (Ill.) Township High School (ETHS). Her primary interests are teaching writing and American literature, particularly African American writers of the Harlem Renaissance and American women writers. Her research interests include classroom gender dynamics, minority student achievement, and teacher-student relationships and their impact on learning. In addition to teaching, she is a staff developer at ETHS, assisting new faculty members in the English department with such issues as classroom management, student/teacher/ parent communication, and content pedagogy and practice. She also teaches a course to preservice teachers at Northwestern University, entitled "Teaching and Learning in Social and Cultural Contexts."

Thomas Fowler-Finn is superintendent of the Fort Wayne (Ind.) Community Schools, an urban district of 32,000 students and 4,000 employees. He began his educational career as a teacher in his hometown of Pittsfield, Massachusetts, and at age twenty-five became a teaching principal in Vermont. He also has served as a supervising principal, assistant superintendent for curriculum and instruction, and a superintendent of schools in New York and Massachusetts. In addition, he has served as a consultant for the Soros Foundation to the government of Albania, launched the first national education summit for mayors and superintendents, served as president of the national organization of Large City School Superintendents, presented at national conferences, written numerous articles, and received local and state recognition for leadership in education. He is the founder and current president of the Network for Equity in Student Achievement, a national organization of urban school districts actively working to close the achievement gap between minority and majority students.

Michelle Galley is a staff writer for *Education Week*, a Washington, DC–based national newspaper that covers schools, as well as state and federal education policy. She writes about philanthropic giving to schools, service learning, school partnerships with community organizations and businesses, and education in the states of Idaho, Oklahoma, and Texas. She has also covered early childhood education, special education, curriculum, and research on boys' academic achievement.

Michael S. Kimmel is professor of sociology at the State University of New York at Stony Brook. His books include *Changing Men* (Sage, 1987), *Men Confront Pornography* (Meridian, 1990), *Men's Lives* (5th ed., Allyn & Bacon, 2000), *Against the Tide: Profeminist Men in the United States, 1776–1990* (Beacon Press, 1992), *The Politics of Manhood* (Temple University Press, 1995), *Manhood in America: A Cultural History* (Free Press, 1996), and *The Gendered Society* (Oxford University Press, 2000). He also edits *Men and Masculinities*, an interdisciplinary scholarly journal, a book series on men and masculinity at the University of California Press, and the Sage Series on Men and Masculinities. He is the spokesperson for the National Organization for Men Against Sexism (NOMAS) and lectures extensively on college campuses in the United States and abroad.

Stacey J. Lee is associate professor of educational policy studies at the University of Wisconsin–Madison. She is the author of *Unraveling the Model Minority Stereotype: Listening to Asian American Youth* (Teachers College Press, 1996). She is also coeditor (with Clara C. Park and A. Lin Goodwin) of the collection *Research on the Education of Asian and Pacific Americans* (Information Age Publishing, 2001). Articles she has authored or co-authored have appeared in such journals as the *Harvard Educational Review*, the *Journal of Negro Education*, *Anthropology and Education Quarterly*, and *Amerasia Journal*. Her research interests focus on the formation of ethnic and racial identities among Asian American high school students.

Arthur Lipkin is an educational consultant and associate editor of the *Journal of Gay and Lesbian Issues in Education*. He was an instructor at the Harvard Graduate School of Education from 1993 to 1999. He also directed the Safe Colleges Program of the Massachusetts Governor's Commission on Gay and Lesbian Youth, the Massachusetts Department of Education's Project for the Integration of Gay and Lesbian

Youth Issues in School Personnel Certification Programs, and Project 10 East at Cambridge Rindge and Latin School in Cambridge, Massachusetts. He is the author of *Beyond Diversity Day: A Q&A on Gay and Lesbian Issues in Schools* (Rowman & Littlefield, in press) and *Understanding Homosexuality, Changing Schools* (Westview Press, 1999). He taught in the Cambridge Public Schools for twenty years.

Michael Nakkula is the Marie and Max Kargman Assistant Professor of Human Development and Urban Education Advancement at the Harvard Graduate School of Education (HGSE). He directs the adolescent focus of HGSE's Risk and Prevention Program, a specialized master's program addressing the interrelationship of risk and resilience as it is manifested in school and other life contexts. He is the co-author (with Sharon Ravitch) of *Matters of Interpretation: Reciprocal Transformation in Therapeutic and Developmental Relationships with Youth* (Jossey-Bass, 1998), which explores how adults and youth change each other through working relationships of various types.

Sonia Nieto is professor of education at the University of Massachusetts at Amherst. She has been a teacher for thirty-five years, teaching students at all levels from elementary through graduate school. Her research focuses on multicultural education; the education of Latinos, immigrants, and other culturally and linguistically diverse students; and Puerto Rican children's literature. Her books include *Affirming Diversity: The Sociopolitical Context of Multicultural Education* (3rd ed., Longman, 2000), *The Light in Their Eyes: Creating Multicultural Learning Communities* (Teachers College Press, 1999), and *Puerto Rican Students in U.S. Schools* (Teachers College Press, 2000). She also has published numerous book chapters and articles in such journals as *Educational Forum,* the *Harvard Educational Review, Multicultural Education,* and *Theory into Practice.* She serves on several national advisory boards that focus on educational equity and social justice, including those of Facing History and Ourselves and Educators for Social Responsibility. She has received many awards for her advocacy and activism, including the 1989 Human and Civil Rights Award from the Massachusetts Teachers Association, the 1995 Drylongso Award for Anti-Racist Activists from Community Change in Boston, the 1996 Teacher of the Year Award from the Hispanic Educators of Massachusetts, and the 1997 Multicultural Educator of the Year Award from NAME, the National Association for Multicultural Education.

Pedro A. Noguera is the Judith K. Dimon Professor of Communities and Schools at the Harvard Graduate School of Education. Previously, he was professor of social and cultural studies at the Graduate School of Education and director of the Institute for the Study of Social Change at the University of California, Berkeley. His research focuses on the ways in which schools respond to social and economic conditions within the urban environment. He has engaged in collaborative research with several large urban school districts, and has published and lectured on topics such as youth violence, race relations within schools, the potential impact of school choice and vouchers on urban public schools, factors contributing to student achievement, and secondary issues resulting from desegregation in public schools. His articles on these topics have appeared in numerous edited volumes and other publications, such as *Educational Leadership, Education and Urban Society*, and *The Nation*. He is the author of *Confronting the Urban: How City Schools Can Respond to Social Inequity* (Teachers College Press, 2003). He was a K–12 classroom teacher for several years and continues to teach part-time at the high school level.

John Raible is a doctoral candidate in language, literacy, and culture at the University of Massachusetts at Amherst. His scholarly interests include racial identity development, transracial adoption, and multicultural education. Previously, he worked for fifteen years as a multicultural educator in public schools in a number of settings, including in New Mexico, California, and New York. At UMass and Westfield State College, John has taught "Introduction to Multicultural Education." He also works as a consultant on cultural identity and adoption and is one of the adult adoptees featured in the film "Struggle for Identity: Issues in Transracial Adoption." John has two sons adopted from foster care.

Michael Sadowski is assistant editor of the *Harvard Education Letter* and winner of the 2002 National Press Club Award for analytical newsletter journalism. He also is an instructor and advanced doctoral candidate at the Harvard Graduate School of Education, where he teaches about lesbian, gay, bisexual, and transgender (LGBT) issues in K–12 education. He is a vice-chair of the Massachusetts Governor's Commission on Gay and Lesbian Youth, a group that advises the governor's office and the Departments of Education and Public Health on policies concerning the welfare and support of LGBT youth in the state's schools and communities. A former English and drama teacher at Dennis-Yarmouth Regional High School on Cape Cod, Michael continues to teach at the high school level in the Cambridge-Harvard Summer Academy, a partnership between Cambridge Rindge and Latin School and the Harvard Graduate School of Education.

Beverly Daniel Tatum, a clinical psychologist, is the president of Spelman College in Atlanta. She is the author of *Why Are All the Black Kids Sitting Together in the Cafeteria? And Other Conversations about Race* (Basic Books, 1997) and *Assimilation Blues: Black Families in a White Community* (Greenwood Press, 1987). She also has written various pieces published in edited books and journals, including "Talking about Race, Learning about Racism: An Application of Racial Identity Development Theory in the Classroom" in the *Harvard Educational Review*. Her areas of expertise include Black families in White America, racial identity in teens, and race in the classroom. Prior to her leadership at Spelman, she was the acting president of Mount Holyoke College, a college for women in South Hadley, Massachusetts, where she also served as dean.

Angela Valenzuela is an associate professor in the department of curriculum and instruction and the Center for Mexican American Studies at the University of Texas at Austin. She previously taught sociology at Rice University in Houston, Texas, and was a visiting scholar at the Center for Mexican American Studies at the University of Houston. Her research and teaching interests are in the sociology of education, minority youth in schools, educational policy, and urban education reform. She is the author of *Subtractive Schooling: U.S.-Mexican Youth and the Politics of Caring* (State University of New York Press, 1999), winner of both the 2000 American Educational Research Association Outstanding Book Award and the 2001 Critics' Choice Award from the American Educational Studies Association. Some of her current work focuses on high-stakes testing policy and Latino youth.

Michael L. Wehmeyer is associate professor of special education, director of the Kansas University Center on Developmental Disabilities, and associate director of the Beach Center on Disability, all at the University of Kansas. His research interests include self-determination for students with disabilities, gender equity in special education, technology use and intellectual disability, and instructional strategies for students with severe, multiple disabilities. His recent publications include *Theory in Self-Determination: Foundations for Educational Practice* (Charles C. Thomas, 2003, with Brian Abery, Dennis Mithaug, and Roger Stancliffe), *Teaching Students with Mental Retardation: Providing Access to the General Curriculum* (Brookes, 2002, with Deanna J. Sands, Earle Knowlton, and Elizabeth B. Kozleski), *Mental Retardation in the 21st Century* (ProEd, 1999, with James Patton), and *Teaching Self-Determination to Students with Disabilities: Basic Skills for Successful Transition* (Brookes, 1997, with Martin Agran and Carolyn Hughes).

Index